PEOPLES
of
AFRICA

Democratic Republic of Congo

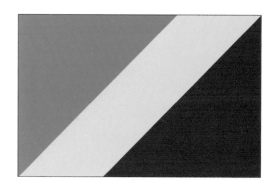

Republic of Congo

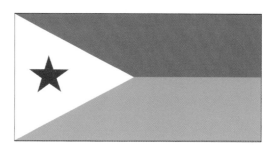

Djibouti

Egypt

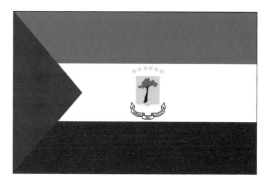

Equatorial Guinea

Eritrea

PEOPLES

of

AFRICA

Volume 3
Congo–Eritrea

MARSHALL CAVENDISH
NEW YORK • LONDON • TORONTO • SYDNEY

Marshall Cavendish Corporation
99 White Plains Road
Tarrytown, New York 10591-9001

Reference Edition 2003

Consultants:
Bryan Callahan, Department of History, Johns Hopkins University
Kevin Shillington

Pronunciation Consultant: Nancy Gratton

Contributing authors:
Fiona Macdonald
Elizabeth Paren
Kevin Shillington
Gillian Stacey
Philip Steele

Discovery Books
Managing Editor: Paul Humphrey
Project Editor: Helen Dwyer
Text Editor: Valerie J. Weber
Design Concept: Ian Winton
Designer: Barry Dwyer
Cartographer: Stefan Chabluk

Marshall Cavendish
Editorial Director: Paul Bernabeo
Editor: Marian Armstrong

The publishers would like to thank the following for their permission to reproduce photographs:
Corbis (Paul Almasy: 128; Paul Velasco/ABPL: 115); Robert Estall Photo Library: (Carol Beckwith/Angela Fisher: 135; Angela Fisher: 116); Mary Evans Picture Library (126, 140); Werner Forman Archive (British Museum, UK: 138; Brooklyn Museum, New York, USA: 112 bottom; Musée Royal Afrique Central, Tervuren, Belgium: 112 top); gettyone Stone: (James Strachan: cover); Hulton Getty Picture Collection (134); Hutchison Library (Sarah Errington: 123, 142; Melanie Friend: 145 top; Carlos Freire: 143; Jeremy Horner: 150 bottom; Mary Jelliffe: 120, 136; Trevor Page: 163); ICCE Photolibrary (Conrad Aveling: 125, 129, 131, 155 top); Panos Pictures (Trygve Bølstad: 145 bottom; J. H. Morris: 139; Caroline Penn: 144; Betty Press: 118; Nick Robinson: 117; Sami Sallinen: 159, 162; Marc Schlossman: 110, 119, 121, 122; Sean Sprague: 151, 155 bottom, 156, 157; Still Pictures (Bojan Brecel: 147; Nigel Dickinson: 150 top; William Fautre: 132; Michel Günther: 124; Jorgen Schytte: 146, 149, 161); Topham Picturepoint (153)

(cover) *An Egyptian man at Luxor in Upper Egypt.*

Editor's note: Many systems of dating have been used by different cultures throughout history. *Peoples of Africa* uses B.C.E. (Before Common Era) and C.E. (Common Era) instead of B.C. (Before Christ) and A.D. (Anno Domini, "In the Year of the Lord") out of respect for the diversity of the world's peoples.

Library of Congress Cataloging-in-Publication Data

Peoples of Africa.
     p. cm.
   Includes bibliographical references and index.
   Contents: v. 1. Algeria–Botswana — v. 2. Burkina–Faso–Comoros — v. 3. Congo, Democratic Republic of–Eritrea — v. 4. Ethiopia–Guinea — v. 5. Guinea-Bissau–Libya — v. 6. Madagascar–Mayotte — v. 7. Morocco–Nigeria — v. 8. Réunion–Somalia — v. 9. South Africa–Tanzania — v. 10. Togo–Zimbabwe — v. 11. Index.
   ISBN 0-7614-7158-8 (set)
     1. Ethnology—Africa—Juvenile literature. 2. Africa—History—Juvenile literature. 3. Africa—Social life and customs—Juvenile literature. I. Marshall Cavendish Corporation.

GN645 .P33 2000
305.8'0096—dc21

                                          99-088550

     ISBN 0-7614-7158-8 (set)
     ISBN 0-7614-7161-8 (vol. 3)

Printed in Hong Kong

06 05 04 03   6 5 4 3 2

Contents

CONGO,
Democratic Republic of

FORMERLY KNOWN AS ZAIRE, THIS LARGE
COUNTRY SPRAWLS ACROSS CENTRAL
AFRICA, bordering nine countries.

Dense, tropical rain forests cover two-thirds of the country, with savanna lands in the south. Its only coastline surrounds the mouth of the Congo River.

Most of the basin of the Congo River lies within the Democratic Republic. The river is fed by the maze of tributaries and streams that drains the rain forests. Wooded regions also line the rivers that cross the drier savanna regions.

CENTRAL
AFRICAN REPUBLIC

SUDAN

Ubangi River

Congo River

Ituri River

Lindi River

Lake Albert

REPUBLIC
OF CONGO

EQUATEUR
Kisangani
Boyoma Falls
RUWENZORI MASSIF

UGANDA
Lake Edward

Mbandaka

CONGO BASIN

Lualaba River

Lake Kivu
Bukavu

RWANDA

DEMOCRATIC
REPUBLIC
OF CONGO

BURUNDI

Kasai River

GREAT RIFT VALLEY

BANDUNDU

TANZANIA

KINSHASA

KASAI

Matadi

Kikwit

MITUMBA MOUNTAINS

Lake
Tanganyika

ATLANTIC
OCEAN

Kananga

Mbuji-Mayi

ANGOLA

SHABA

Lake
Mweru

ZAMBIA

N

Lubumbashi

miles 0   200
km 0   300

In the east the Mitumba Mountains rise from the depression formed by the Congo Basin. The country's eastern border lies on a western branch of the Great Rift Valley. This deep crack in the earth's crust is marked by long lakes such as Lake Tanganyika and volcanic peaks such as the Ruwenzori Massif, which rises to 16,794 feet (5,119 meters).

A boat on a bank of the Congo River, near Mbandaka (uhm-bahn-DAH-kah), chief town of the Equateur region. Clumps of water hyacinth float in the brown water.

A Land of Forests

The earliest inhabitants of the Congo (KAHNG-goe) region were probably the ancestors of today's Mbuti (ehm-BOO-tee) and Efe (EH-fae) peoples. They lived by hunting the wild animals of the vast rain forests of the Congo Basin. They gathered fruits, roots, and leaves and used smoke to drive wild bees from their hives in hollow trees to obtain sweet honeycombs.

Between about three thousand and one thousand years ago, Bantu-speaking (BAN-too) peoples from western and central Africa moved eastward and southward (see CAMEROON). These farmers and fishers acquired copper- and ironworking skills about two thousand years ago. They built villages along the banks of the great rivers and cultivated yams. The forest people came to barter with them, exchanging labor for tools and forest foods for farm crops.

FACTS AND FIGURES

Official name: *République Démocratique du Congo*

Status: *Independent state*

Capital: *Kinshasa*

Major towns: *Lubumbashi, Mbuji-Mayi, Kisangani, Kananga, Bukavu, Kikwit, Matadi*

Area: *905,356 square miles (2,344,872 square kilometers)*

Population: *50,500,000*

Population density: *56 per square mile (22 per square kilometer)*

Peoples: *Over 200 ethnic groups; the largest are the Kongo, Mongo, Luba, Lulua, Shi, Nande, Azande, Chokwe, Ngombe, and Ngala*

Official language: *French*

Currency: *New Zaire*

National day: *Independence Day (June 30)*

Country's name: *The name Congo comes from the Bantu kingdom of Kongo.*

CLIMATE

The Congo Basin is hot and rainy for most of the year. The savanna region's dry season lasts from June to September, while the far north's shorter dry season lasts from December to February. The climate in the east varies with the altitude, with snow falling on the highest mountain peaks.

	Kinshasa	**Lubumbashi**
Average January temperature:	*79°F (26°C)*	*72°F (22°C)*
Average July temperature:	*73°F (23°C)*	*61°F (16°C)*
Average annual precipitation:	*45 in. (114 cm)*	*50 in. (127 cm)*

About seven hundred years ago, the most powerful Bantu group was the Kongo, who extended their kingdom across the Congo River from the north. By the 1400s their Kongo Empire included much of what is now Angola, the coastal regions of the two modern Congo nations, and Gabon. The ruler of this state was called *manikongo* (mah-nee-KAWN-goe), and he lived in great splendor. The empire was organized into regions, each with a governor who was responsible for collecting taxes on traded goods such as

---

Time line:	Forest peoples inhabit central Africa	Bantu-speaking farmers spread through forest	Bantu farmers learn ironworking skills and spread through central and southern Africa	Probable founding of the powerful Kongo kingdom
	ca. 1000 B.C.E.	**ca. 500 B.C.E.**	**ca. 1 C.E.**	**1300s**

Nearly 17 inches (43 centimeters) tall, this statue is carved from soapstone. Figures like this were placed on important Kongo graves in the 1700s and 1800s.

ivory or cloth. Shells were used as currency.

In 1482 the Portuguese arrived at the mouth of the Congo River. They were the first of many European peoples who would have such a devastating impact on the region and on Africa as a whole over the following five hundred years. The Portuguese named the estuary Zaire from a local word *Zadi* (ZAH-dee), meaning "great river," and sent ambassadors to the Manikongo in his capital at M'banza (uhm-BAHN-zah) Congo. The great Kongo Empire soon fell under Portuguese control and became partially Christian.

The Kongo were not the only Bantu people to establish kingdoms in the region. The kingdom of the Luba (LOO-bah) emerged around 1300 and over the next century became a powerful, centralized state. The Luba traced their descent from a great chief called Kalala Ilunga, and their warlike customs were symbolized by their ruler's badge of authority, a carved wooden stand to hold his bow. In the 1450s some of the Luba nobles who had challenged the

ruler's power moved with their followers toward what is now Angola, and set up a rival state called Lunda (LOON-dah) in the 1600s. Another successful state was that of the Kuba (KOO-bah), whose royal clan was called Bushoong (buh-SHOONG), meaning "men of lightning." Their symbol was the throwing knife. These states continued to exist through the 1600s. Soon the small statues for which the region was famous were portraying new weapons—rifles, traded from the Europeans.

Among all the metalworking Bantu peoples, iron was admired and believed to have an almost magical quality. Kuba legends told of a blacksmith king called Mbop Pelyeeng. Legendary Luba hero Chibinda Ilunga is said to have taught metalworking skills to the Chokwe (SHOE-kwae) people in the south.

Central Africa was the birthplace of many rich customs and traditions, but the curse of the slave trade soon devastated the area. The Kongo and some other indigenous peoples already traded in slaves, but they sold only criminals and prisoners captured

This wooden statue represents Mbomboosh, ninety-first king of the Kuba people. He reigned in about 1650, but this figure may have been carved in the 1700s.

Rise of Luba state	Portuguese reach mouth of Congo River	Slave trade develops	Rise of Lunda state	Zanzibari slave traders in east of country	Berlin Conference gives Congo Free State to King Leopold II of Belgium as a personal possession
1300s	**1482**	**1500s**	**1600s**	**1850s**	**1884–1885**

during wars. During the 1500s and 1600s, the Europeans transformed the slave trade by providing a trans-Atlantic connection between Africa and the Americas and launching raids in the interior of Africa. They shipped hundreds of thousands of people to the "New World" as slaves. Slave traders from Portugal, France, Great Britain, and the Netherlands all operated along the western coasts of central Africa. This cruel business lasted well into the 1800s.

The eastern part of the present day Democratic Republic of Congo lay on the trading routes of Nyamwezi (nee-ahm-WAE-zee) and Swahili (swah-HEE-lee) merchants from eastern Africa, who traded in ivory and copper as well as slaves. In the 1850s Swahili and Arab traders settled in the eastern part of the country to send slaves back to the markets of Zanzibar (ZAN-zuh-bahr), an island off the east African coast (see TANZANIA). The captives were treated with great cruelty. People who worked with the Zanzibari Arabs, such as the Yeke (YEH-kae) people, profited from the trade, and founded an empire in the Shaba (Katanga) region.

From Free State to Colony

Portuguese power lay south of the great forests, in what is now Angola, while the Congo Basin, the heart of the continent, remained unknown and feared by the Europeans. All that changed after 1877, when Europeans, traveling from the east, navigated the length of the Lualaba (loo-ah-LAH-bah) and Congo Rivers all the way to the Atlantic Ocean.

King Leopold II of Belgium wanted to develop the area of the Congo Basin as a possible colony, so at the Berlin Conference (1884–1885) the Congo Free State was created. The boundaries of the Congo Free State were drawn up by Europeans who had little knowledge of the region's geography or its many peoples.

The new state was set up as the personal property of the Belgian king and may have been the most brutally administered territory in all of Africa's colonial history. Leopold allowed the International Africa Company to exploit the territory, its people, and resources any way the company desired. This company forced the indigenous people to harvest wild rubber. Rubber harvesters who failed to meet their quotas had their hands chopped off. Many thousands died. International protests against such brutalities grew. By 1908 the Belgian government had taken over the administration of the Congo Free State from Leopold, and the territory became the colony of the Belgian Congo.

Under Belgian rule, mining engineers moved in, and diamonds, gold, and copper were extracted and exported. Roads and dams were built. However, the indigenous peoples of the region were largely neglected. Education and health care were minimal and were provided mostly by Roman Catholic missionaries. The Belgians banned political parties and deliberately encouraged ethnic conflicts between the many peoples to avoid a united opposition to Belgian rule. During World War II (1939–1945), the Belgian Congo supported the Allies (including Great Britain, the

Growing trade in rubber, using brutal forced labor	Belgium takes over territory and renames it Belgian Congo	Heavy rioting in Kinshasa	Independence; Katanga district attempts to break away; civil war ensues	Katanga separatists defeated
1890s	**1908**	**1959**	**1960**	**1963**

United States, and Canada) and provided valuable raw materials for the war effort. During the 1950s the economy in the Belgian Congo boomed, and Belgian colonials settled down to enjoy a wealthy lifestyle, but their dreams of peacefully exploiting the country were soon shattered.

In 1958 the French granted self-government to Congo-Brazzaville, the Belgian Congo's neighboring territory on the northern bank of the Congo River. The taste for freedom soon spread southward, and Léopoldville, now Kinshasa (kin-SHAH-suh), the capital of the Belgian Congo, erupted into riots. The Belgian authorities had done little to prepare people for independence or to train them for work in government or industry. For example, there was no higher education for black Africans before 1954.

The Years of Chaos

When independence did come in 1960, with Patrice Lumumba elected as the first prime minister, celebrations were short-lived. Conflict immediately arose between those political parties that supported a strong centralist state, with power concentrated in the federal government, and those that represented the regions. The mineral-rich southern province of Katanga, later renamed Shaba (SHAH-buh), declared it was breaking away from the new country. A politician named Moise Tshombe, who supported Belgian mining interests in Katanga, led the secession. Lumumba called in the United Nations and, in increasing desperation, Soviet (Russian)

troops. A bitter civil war followed, which ended with the assassination of Lumumba, the expulsion of the Soviets, the formation of a government of national unity, and by 1963, an end to the Katanga secession. However, later that year, the country broke up in civil war once again as the centralists attacked the coalition government. Belgian soldiers and mercenaries joined the government forces to defeat the centralists. With elections due to be held, an army general named Joseph-Désiré Mobutu, backed by the United States and most European countries, seized power.

Mobutu remained in power from 1965 until 1997. He renamed the country Zaire and made it into a ruthless, one-party state. When copper prices collapsed in the 1970s, Mobutu nationalized foreign-owned industries to raise state revenues. Zaire became increasingly corrupt and chaotic, while Mobutu banked a personal fortune of over $6 billion in his own accounts. Throughout the Cold War years, he received the support of the United States and its allies on the grounds that he was anticommunist and would guarantee that Zaire's rich mineral reserves would be exported to them and not to the Soviet Union and other communist countries.

However, in the 1990s Mobutu began to lose his grip on power. With the collapse of the communist Soviet Union, he was no longer useful in Cold War politics. Many other countries objected to Mobutu's severe human rights abuses and withdrew their aid to Zaire. Inflation soared in 1995. As Rwanda and Burundi erupted into a series of terrible conflicts, refugees poured

Belgian troops called in to defeat separatists in central and eastern Congo	Joseph-Désiré Mobutu seizes power with backing of Western nations	One-party state emerges, ruled by Mobutu's Popular Revolutionary Movement	Country renamed Zaire	Mobutu seizes foreign-owned businesses
1964	**1965**	**1970**	**1971**	**1974**

across Zaire's eastern border (see RWANDA and BURUNDI).

In the chaos that followed, rebel groups banded together under the command of Rwandan officers and speedily marched westward. Laurent Kabila emerged as leader of the anti-Mobutu movement that swept the country. Kabila, a leading rebel in the 1960s, had spent most of the intervening years in exile and was little known to most Congolese. Mobutu was overthrown in May 1997, and the country was renamed the Democratic Republic of Congo.

Kabila immediately banned all political parties and vaguely promised elections sometime in the future. By 1998 the country had plunged back into renewed strife.

By 1994, protests against Mobutu were becoming common. Here, demonstrators appeal to South African leader Nelson Mandela for help.

Although this was a civil war, it appeared it might divide a vast region of Africa. As alliances shifted, Kabila was supported by Zimbabwe, Namibia, Chad, Angola, Sudan, and Libya. The new rebels were backed by Uganda, Rwanda, and many Congolese dissidents. Peace deals were struck between most of the countries concerned during 1999. However, international troops remained, fighting continued in some areas, and a lasting peaceful settlement still seemed some way off.

Diversity in Languages and Beliefs

The Democratic Republic of Congo is home to a dozen or so larger ethnic groups and about 190 smaller ones, with a similar number of languages and dialects. French

Security forces kill democracy campaigners; Belgium stops aid	Mobutu forced to end one-party state	Crisis involving Rwandan refugees; civil war	Mobutu overthrown; Laurent Kabila president; Zaire becomes Democratic Republic of Congo	Rebels fight Kabila's forces
1990	**1991**	**1996**	**1997**	**1998**

is still the official language, as it was in the days of the Belgian Congo. Lingala is the chief language of Kinshasa and central regions. In the west, Kongo is widely spoken. Central and southern districts are home to the Luba languages. Nandé is heard in northeastern parts and Swahili in the far east; Swahili was introduced in the 1700s and 1800s by traders from the east African coast.

The Kongo, descendants of the founders of the Kongo Empire, live in the western part of the country, around the Congo River. Their traditional homeland extends northward along the coast of the Congo Republic and southward into Angola. They are a Bantu people and work as farmers and fishers and as industrial workers in the cities. The Mongo (MAWN-goe) are mostly farmers who live in the forests of the central region. The southeast is dominated by the Luba, who form three main groups:

This Mangbetu elder wears a raffia hat and a leopard's tooth necklace. His fly whisk is made of elephant's tail hair. The Mangbetu are famed for their woodcarving.

Let's Talk Lingala

Lingala is based on a Bantu language, Bobangi, but it has adopted many French words. It is the chief medium for Congolese pop music.

mbote (uhm-BOE-tae)	*good morning*
sango nini (san-goh NEE-nee)	*how are you?*
natondi yo (nah-TON-dee yoe)	*thank you*
palado (pah-lah-DOE)	*please*
limbisa ngai? (LEEM-bee-sah uhn-GAH-ee)	*where are you going?*

---

the Luba-Hemba (LOO-bah HEM-bah), the Luba-Bambo (LOO-bah BAHM-boe), and the Luba-Shankaji (LOO-bah shan-KAH-jee). Long ago they built their wealth on copper mining and trading. In modern times they dominated the economic and political life of Shaba (Katanga) but suffered some persecution under Mobutu.

The Chokwe-Lunda peoples of the far south are farmers of the savanna, whose homelands stretch into Angola and Zambia (see ANGOLA and ZAMBIA). The Azande (uh-ZAHN-dee) and Mangbetu (mahng-BAE-too) peoples live in the north and northeast, near the Sudanese border. The

People of the Forest

The Mbuti are one of the central African peoples of slight build; most adults are between four feet, six inches (1.37 meters) and five feet, two inches (1.57 meters) tall. They live in the dense forests around the Ituri (ee-TOO-ree) and Lindi (LIN-dee) Rivers. The men hunt for game, such as antelope, porcupine, and rodents, using spears, nets, snares, and bows and poison arrows. The women gather berries, fruits, and insect larvae. They spend much of the year deep in the forest, forming hunting bands with about fifteen to forty members. The band has no chief, and each band member is treated like a member of the same family.

Sometimes the Mbuti visit the farming villages of neighboring Bantu peoples, such as the Bira, the Ltsi, and the Ndaka. They barter goods and produce with these peoples, but the relationship goes much deeper than that. They also share religious ceremonies and rituals such as circumcision and are respected by the farmers, who believe the Mbuti are in touch with the mysteries and spirits of the great forest. The Mbuti no longer speak their own language but have adopted the Bantu languages of their neighbors.

In the years since independence, loggers, miners, soldiers, and tourists have invaded the Ituri forest. The Mbuti call themselves bamiki ba'ndura (bah-MIH-kee bahn-DOO-rah), meaning "children of the forest," but their way of life in the forest is being threatened like never before.

The ancestors of this Mbuti boy lived in the forests of the Congo Basin thousands of years ago, but today his land and way of life are threatened.

northeast is also home to the Alur (AH-loor) and Lugbara (luhg-BAH-rah), who also live across the border in Uganda (see UGANDA).

Most of the region's peoples are subdivided into clans, groups who claim descent from a common ancestor. Clans are made up of individual families that follow an extended pattern, including grandparents, aunts, uncles, and cousins. The oldest male often heads the family. In recent years, as people have moved from their villages to the cities or have been scattered by political upheavals, many of these relationships have broken up.

These Kinshasa men are present-day Kimbanguistes. Born around 1889, Simon Kimbangu broke away from the Baptists to form an African-based church. He died in 1951.

Fetishes and Magic

Traditional healing and magic rituals are widely practiced, especially among the peoples of the far west—the Kongo, Yomba, and Vili—and the Songye of the east. These peoples make small statues called fetishes in an attempt to ward off the forces of evil. Fetishes may take the form of a human or an animal. Some larger fetishes are pierced with iron nails. When a nail is driven into the fetish it is believed to activate a spell requested by a member of the tribe. Smaller fetishes are adorned with cloth, feathers, or fur. Early Christian missionaries from Europe mistakenly believed that Africans worshiped images such as these fetishes, and the missionaries destroyed them as "the work of the devil."

Over half of the population is Christian, primarily Roman Catholic, but there are also many Protestants. Some of these are members of the Church of Jesus Christ on Earth, a movement founded in the Belgian Congo by Simon Kimbangu in 1921. They are known as *Kimbanguistes* (keem-BAHN-geests). There are also a number of Muslims. The rest of the population follow traditional African beliefs. These beliefs share a reverence for life forces in the form of spirits, a respect for one's ancestors, the practice of magic, healing, and fortune-telling, and sometimes the belief in a single creator god. The forms of belief or worship vary greatly from one ethnic group to another. Ceremonies and rituals, masked dances and drumming mark rites of passage such as coming-of-age.

Fufu and Saka-saka

A Congolese meal is very filling. It is most commonly based on rice; fufu *(foo-FOO), which is a stiff cornmeal porridge similar to Italian polenta; or* kwanga *(KWAHN-gah), which is mashed yams or cassava. These ingredients are topped by a hot, spicy sauce such as* moambé *(muh-WAHM-bae), which is made of peanuts and palm oil.* Saka-saka *(sah-kah SAH-kah) is a stew of cassava leaves. Chicken is often made into a stew as well. River fish include a local form of perch. Hunting for food is still common, and a menu of meats from the wild might include monkey, antelope, crocodile, or porcupine.*

The trip from Kinshasa to Kisangani by river steamer can take up to twelve days. As the riverboat chugs upstream, women cook plantains, cassava, or fish on the deck.

Diamonds in the Dust

The Democratic Republic of Congo should be one of the wealthiest regions of Africa. It is one of the world's biggest producers of industrial-grade diamonds. The country's natural resources include copper, gold, silver, uranium, zinc, tin, and manganese; it also has oil and 65 percent of the world's cobalt reserves. The country is also capable of generating more hydroelectric power than any other country in Africa.

However, the new country still suffers from the effects of colonial exploitation and from chronic corruption and mismanagement during the years of independence. It is crippled with debt.

Not surprisingly, minerals make up 85 percent of the country's export wealth. Coffee is a major export. Other cash crops include cocoa, tea, rubber, cotton, rice,

peanuts, palm oil, and sugarcane. The chief agricultural area is the southern savanna. It is also the region where most grazing takes place. The great forests, which make up half of all of Africa's remaining woodlands, produce precious hardwoods such as mahogany and ebony.

Farming and Food

About 68 percent of the labor force works the land, but most of the production is at a subsistence level, meeting village and family needs alone—and it barely does that. Basic foods must be imported. Poor diets mean that malnutrition is common. Most country dwellers have small plots of land

119

where they grow cassava (a starchy root crop), corn, and plantains (large bananas used in cooking). Land is often cultivated on a shifting basis; it's abandoned for newly cleared plots when the soil is exhausted every two or three years. Men clear the land, but women do the majority of planting and harvesting and sell the surplus produce at the local market.

Health and Education

Children are supposed to receive six years of elementary schooling, but the state education system has been disastrously neglected by the government and disrupted by civil war and economic problems. Many elementary schools are run by the Roman Catholic Church, and this has resulted in a relatively high literacy rate for Africa: 84 percent of men and 61 percent of women are able to read and write. There are four universities and many graduate schools.

The country faces severe health care problems. There is only one doctor for every 15,150 people, and in 1996 the mortality rate for children under five was 131 per 1,000. Life expectancy is forty-seven for men and fifty-two for women. Malaria is widespread and in many areas is resistant to chloroquine, the usual preventive medicine. AIDS is widespread. Diseases are made worse by poor water supplies and insufficient urban services such as refuse collection and waste disposal.

Everyday Life in Town and Country

Sixty percent of the Democratic Republic of Congo's population are country dwellers, living in small villages. Homes are often made of mud brick or mud and timber.

Rectangular homes, with roofs of thatch or grooved iron, against a backdrop of lush, green countryside. This is a Kavumba village in the far east of the country.

Congolese Rhythms

Congolese popular music was born in Kinshasa, but it is heard over large areas of central Africa, from Kenya to Nigeria. It has made a great impression outside the continent too. It is sometimes referred to as soukous (SOO-koos), after a dance craze of the 1960s, but in fact there are many different styles. Much of the music in these styles swings along to a rhythm based on the Latin American rumba, which was itself influenced by the music of African slaves. These rhythms are mixed with modern rock styles. The Congo sound is typified by high, tinkling, intricate riffs on the electric guitar. Its founding father was Franco Luambo Makiadi, known simply as Franco, who formed the band OK Jazz in 1956. Franco's death in 1989 was marked by four days of national mourning. Other great international stars have included Tabu Ley "Seigneur" Rochereau, Dr. Nico Kasanda, Kanda Bongo Man, and Mbilia Bel, a female singer, whose beautiful, haunting voice is instantly recognized across the continent.

They are mostly rectangular in design and are roofed with sheet metal or thatch. Round huts with conical roofs are the style in the far north and in the province of Shaba. Deep in the forests, the homes of the Mbuti are small domes or simple sloping shelters made of branches and palm fronds.

The most densely populated region is the industrial province of Shaba. Congolese cities have grown rapidly in the last forty years, as poor villagers from rural areas seek, but rarely find, their fortune on the urban streets. About 35 percent of the workforce remains unemployed. The capital, Kinshasa, is a busy, sprawling city with some 4,500,000 inhabitants—the largest French-speaking city outside France. Here, old colonial buildings and bungalows line broad, tree-lined

A woman with a typical Congolese hairstyle walks to market near the town of Mbuji-Mayi (uhm-BOO-jee-mie-ee). She carries all her goods in a bundle on her head—topped by a rooster.

avenues. The suburbs are crowded and bustling, with concrete apartment buildings and smaller, cheaper homes. There are also quarters of shacks and makeshift housing. Bars and nightclubs abound, both of which play the local pop music that has become popular throughout the continent.

As in other African countries, life in both country and town revolves around the market square. Goods for sale are spread out on the ground and may include anything from rice and peanuts to bales of cloth, sunglasses, wristwatches, batteries, chickens, or dried fish. Many of the market traders are women.

Cities and towns are linked by one of the worst road systems in Africa, with few surfaced highways. It can easily take a month to cross the country overland. The roads are muddy and rutted, regularly washed away by torrential rains. Accidents are common. The rivers have been the main means of transportation for centuries, and the Congo River and its tributaries remain the country's most used thoroughfares. Small dugout canoes, or pirogues, are still used for fishing and trading, and large, slow riverboats, similar to those used on the Nile River in neighboring

Sudan, ply the larger waterways. Several vessels or barges may be pulled by the main steamer, allowing room for a thousand or more passengers, most of whom sleep and camp on the deck. Goods are sold, food is cooked, radios blare pop music. Each riverboat is like a small town in itself.

Wooden traps are the traditional method of catching fish near the Boyoma (formerly Stanley) Falls, on the Congo River near Kisangani.

122

Powerful Art, Fine Crafts

The region occupied by today's Congo nations includes some of the most impressive, beautiful, and powerful woodcarving on the continent. Ritual masks in European collections had a direct influence on modern artists such as Pablo Picasso. Central African artists worked less often in gold and ivory than western Africans, but there are beautiful ivory headrests made by the Luba. These held up the elaborate hairdos of noble women while they slept.

The Mangbetu people of the northeast are famous for a style of modeled terra-cotta (fired pottery) based on geometric designs and long, elegantly sculpted heads. The style dates back to the 1890s. Beautifully carved human figures also adorn traditional Mangbetu harps, made of polished wood and hide.

Heavy wooden face masks, made by the Songye (SAWNG-yeh) people (of the Luba group), are grooved and painted black and white. They were used by chiefs in ceremonies and are often copied today as tourist souvenirs. The Songye and the Hembe (HEM-bee), another people within the Luba grouping, also made ceremonial wooden stools for chiefs, with the seats supported by finely carved human figures.

The Kuba immortalized each of their kings with a fine portrait figure carved in wood. Figures of 19 out of Kuba's 124 known kings have survived. Royal power was also displayed by the wearing of masks made of cowrie shells, raffia, fur, beads, and wood.

These dancers at a coming-of-age ceremony wear raffia costumes as well as masks. They belong to the Pende people, who live east of the capital, in the Bandundu (bahn-DOON-doo) region.

During the 1970s President Mobutu encouraged a program of Africanization, or rejection of colonial attitudes. People were encouraged to get rid of Christian names and adopt African ones. Africanization extended to dress, too, but did not signal a return to the traditional costumes of pre-colonial times. Instead, a style of practical simplicity and lack of formality developed. Today most Congolese men wear T-shirts or casual shirts with trousers, while most women wear cotton dresses or long skirts with blouses.

CONGO, Republic of

FORMERLY KNOWN AS CONGO-BRAZZAVILLE, this country lies to the north of the Congo River. It has a short coastline on the Atlantic Ocean.

The Republic of Congo lies on the equator. From the sandy coastal strip, the land rises to highlands in the Niari region. To the east of the fertile Niari River Valley rises the dry, mostly barren Batéké Plateau. In the north this descends to the basin of the Congo River, with its swamps and dense rain forests. The northeastern border lies on the Ubangi River, one of the major tributaries of the Congo.

CENTRAL AFRICAN REPUBLIC

CAMEROON

Motaba River

Ubangi River

Sangha River

Mbomo

REPUBLIC

Likouala River

OF

GABON

CONGO

CONGO BASIN

Congo River

DEMOCRATIC REPUBLIC OF CONGO

BATÉKÉ PLATEAU

NIARI

Niari River

ATLANTIC OCEAN

Loubomo

Nkayi

Kouilou River

BRAZZAVILLE

Malebo Pool

Pointe-Noire

CABINDA (ANGOLA)

N

miles 0 — 100
km 0 — 150

The whine of chainsaws shatters the peace of the rain forest in the Congo Basin. Just over half the land in the Republic of Congo is covered in forests and woodlands.

CLIMATE

The Republic of Congo is mostly hot and humid. A long dry season extends from May to September, and a shorter one occurs from mid-December to mid-January. The long rains last from mid-January to mid-May and the short rains from October to mid-December. Rainfall is high in the Congo Basin but lower on the plateau and the coast, which is kept cool by ocean currents.

Average January temperature: *78°F (26°C)*

Average July temperature: *73°F (23°C)*

Average annual precipitation: *59 in. (150 cm)*

Peoples North of the Great River

The first peoples to inhabit the region north of the Congo (KAHNG-goe) River moved through the great rain forests, hunting wild animals and gathering food. They were probably the ancestors of small-statured groups such as the Baka (bah-KAH) and the Binga (BEEN-gah)

Around 500 B.C.E., Bantu-speakers (BAN-too) began to enter the region, mostly from the north. They were farmers, who built villages on the savanna and the riverbanks. By two thousand years ago, they had learned the skills of ironworking and developed relatively advanced agricultural tools. They bartered with the Baka in the forest, exchanging crops for useful tools, and hunted game such as antelope. The two groups did not

Baka families gather on the Motaba River in the far north of the Republic of Congo. These forest dwellers are descendants of the first inhabitants of the country.

FACTS AND FIGURES

Official name: *République du Congo*

Status: *Independent state*

Capital: *Brazzaville*

Major towns: *Pointe-Noire, Nkayi, Loubomo*

Area: *132,046 square miles (342,000 square kilometers)*

Population: *2,700,000*

Population density: *20 per square mile (8 per square kilometer)*

Peoples: *48 percent Kongo; 20 percent Sangha; 17 percent Teke; 12 percent Mboshi; and many other small groups*

Official language: *French*

Currency: *CFA franc*

National days: *The Three Glorious Days (August 13–15)*

Country's name: *The name Congo comes from the Bantu kingdom of Kongo.*

intermarry, which is why the Baka remained of small stature.

Powerful Bantu kingdoms developed in the region in the Middle Ages. Loango (luh-WANG-goe), the kingdom of the Vili (VEE-lee) people, developed on the coast around Pointe-Noire (pwehnt-NWAHR) in the 1200s. The Vili regarded their kings as gods. Loango soon fell under the overall rule of the mighty Kongo Empire, which rose to power between the 1100s and 1400s. This was a federation of chiefdoms, whose

Time line:	Forest peoples inhabit central Africa	Bantu-speaking farmers spread through forest	Founding of the Loango kingdom	Expansion of the Kongo kingdom
	ca. 1000 B.C.E.	ca. 500 B.C.E.	ca. 1200	1300s

overall ruler held the title *manikongo* (mah-nee-KAWN-goe). Its territory stretched southward across the Congo River (see CONGO, DEMOCRATIC REPUBLIC OF, and ANGOLA). The center of its power lay in northern Angola.

Another powerful kingdom was that of the Teke (TAE-kae) peoples of the plateau region, north of Malebo (mah-LAE-boe) Pool. This kingdom emerged as a confederation of nomadic peoples in a lightly populated part of the country. During the seventeenth and eighteenth centuries, the Teke kingdom grew powerful from mining iron and copper and trading them at the great market crossroads of Malebo Pool, an expansion of the Congo River.

This picture of the Loango capital was drawn by a Dutch explorer around 1670. The city appears to have been a mile or so across and defended by a long palisade.

Slave Trading and Europeans

In 1482 the Portuguese reached the mouth of the Congo River. They had been exploring the African coast in search of gold and sea routes to India. They made contact with the Manikongo in his court at M'banza (uhm-BAHN-zah) Congo and soon were building forts and sending in Roman Catholic missionaries.

The coastal peoples of central Africa had long traded captives taken in wars in the interior of the continent. During the 1500s the Portuguese took full advantage of this trade, purchasing slaves from the local peoples and shipping them to the Americas. They were kept in wretched conditions and many perished on the long voyage.

The slave trade benefited some local peoples. The Loango kingdom grew wealthy enough to break away from

Portuguese reach the mouth of the Congo River	Portuguese develop slave trade; Loango kingdom breaks away from Kongo	Coast claimed as French Congo; Teke kingdom becomes a French protectorate	Berlin Conference recognizes French claim to interior of region
1482	**1500s**	**1880**	**1885**

Kongo. However, the overall effect of the trade was disastrous. The population of western central Africa shrank dramatically, and its culture was almost destroyed. It was 1830 before the slave trade was outlawed, but further terrors lay ahead for the peoples of central Africa, as European powers eagerly set out to take over Africa.

The Colonial Era

From 1875 to 1888, a Frenchman named Pierre Savorgnan de Brazza explored the Congo, and in 1880 he claimed the coastal region for France. This was a strategic move that helped France counterbalance Belgium's growing influence south of the Congo River. The Teke kingdom became a French protectorate, and in 1885 the Berlin Conference recognized French claims to the interior of the region as well.

In 1903 the French Congo became known as Moyen-Congo (Mid-Congo), and five years later it became part of the wider territory of French Equatorial Africa, with Brazzaville (BRAH-zuh-veel) as its capital. The forced labor system introduced by the French was no better than slavery. Men were driven from their villages on the plateaus at gunpoint and forced to harvest wild rubber hundreds of miles away, among the malarial swamps of the Congo Basin. Back home, farming plots went untended. As a result, terrible famines raged from 1914 onward.

Many Congolese sought comfort from their misery in religion, joining the Church of Jesus Christ on Earth, a movement founded in the Belgian Congo by Simon

Hell's Railroad

Large stretches of the Congo and Ubangi (oo-BANG-gee) Rivers are navigable, but access from the ocean is blocked by an impassable series of rapids on the lower river. The French decided that the only way to fully exploit equatorial Africa was to bypass the rapids with a railroad from the interior of the country to the ocean. In 1924 this engineering project, the Congo-Ocean Railroad, began. It was hailed as a marvelous example of European engineering skills.

The French forced thousands of laborers from all over equatorial Africa to build the railroad. People were driven from their homes to work and die on the project. It has been claimed that a life was lost for each tie laid. The work took fourteen years to complete. The railroad is still a key to the economic survival of the Republic of Congo and the Central African Republic, but it was built at a terrible cost to humanity.

Kimbangu in 1921. Five years later political opposition to colonialism was born in the French Equatorial Africa Association. In 1939 Simon Pierre M'Padi, claiming to be a successor to Kimbangu, started another indigenous religious movement.

After World War II (1939–1945), the French conceded increasing degrees of home rule, with full independence being achieved in 1960.

1946	1960	1963	1970	1979
Self-rule; representation in French parliament	Full independence as Congo-Brazzaville; Fulbert Youlou president	Youlou overthrown; National Revolutionary Movement becomes sole political party	Communist state declared	Coup brings Denis Sassou-Nguesso to power

communist republic in 1970. The Congolese Workers' Party became the sole political party. In 1979 it chose Denis Sassou-Nguesso, an army officer, as president. In 1990, as the communist governments in central and eastern Europe collapsed, the Congo formally returned to capitalist economics.

Multiparty elections were held in 1992, bringing Pascal Lissouba to power, amid accusations of election fraud by the opposition parties. In 1995 a broader-based government of national unity was elected, but bitter fighting between rival militias dominated life around the capital in the late 1990s. Troops loyal to Lissouba clashed with those loyal to former president Sassou-Nguesso. Attempts to bring the latter into the official armed forces failed, and by 1997 a full-scale civil war was raging around Brazzaville. In October of that year, Lissouba was forced into exile, and many of his supporters fled to the Democratic Republic of Congo. Sassou-Nguesso became president once again.

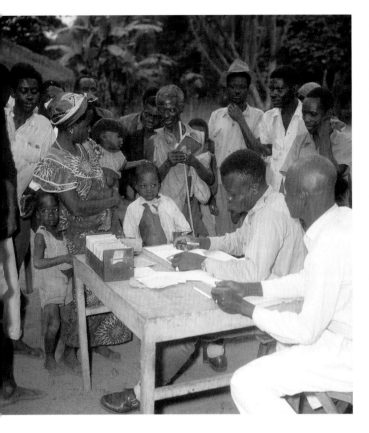

Villagers wait their turn to be registered by officials at a census organized by the French authorities in 1957, just three years before the country became independent.

Troubled Times

The first president of Congo-Brazzaville was a Roman Catholic priest named Fulbert Youlou. He was pro-French and a moderate. However, his government was corrupt and rapidly became despised. A popular movement arose that pushed for socialist politics. In 1963 Youlou was forced from office, and the National Revolutionary Movement took power.

In the following years the government of Congo-Brazzaville became more left-wing amid a series of coups, assassinations, and political executions. The country became a

Peoples and Beliefs

The largest ethnic group today are the Kongo. They mostly live west and southwest of Brazzaville, and closely related groups of them still live in the south, in the Democratic Republic of Congo and Angolan territory (see CONGO, DEMOCRATIC REPUBLIC OF, and ANGOLA). They have always been market traders and farmers. The Vili people mostly live along the coast, fishing and working in the port of Pointe-Noire. The Teke (TAE-kae)

Country renamed Republic of Congo	Multiparty elections; Pascal Lissouba becomes president	Government of national unity elected	Civil war; Lissouba replaced by Sassou-Nguesso
1991	**1992**	**1995**	**1997**

people, traditionally hunters and fishers, occupy the plateau region to the north of Brazzaville. Peoples of the forests include the Sangha (SAHN-gah), farmers and hunters, and the Mboshi (uhm-BOE-shee), fishers from settlements in the region of the Likouala River. The Kota (KOE-tah) people, famous woodcarvers, live in the north and west of the country. Most Kota live across the border in Gabon (see GABON). While many members of these groups still follow their traditional lifestyles, other members live and work in towns. Brazzaville and other cities have sizable European populations as well.

Most of the Congo's inhabitants are speakers of Bantu languages. Lingala, a language which originated in the Ubangi River region and was influenced by French, is today widely spoken in the north and east, and as far south as Brazzaville. To the south and west, down

Relics of the Past

A belief in magic and in the living spirits of one's ancestors contributed to the making of reliquaries, caskets to hold the bones of the dead. Among the Mbede (uhm-BAE-dae), a people living near the Gabon border, and their southern neighbors, the Kuyu (KOO-yoo), the bones of great hunters were placed inside small statues of carved wood. The combination of image and relics was believed to possess potent magic and could produce awe and terror in anyone who looked at it. The reliquaries also conferred great status and power on their owners.

Standing knee-deep in water, a fisherman casts his net into the Mambili River, a tributary of the Congo that flows through forests in the northwest.

to Pointe-Noire, people speak Munukutuba (moo-noo-kuh-TOO-buh), a dialect of Kongo. French is retained as the official language of government and is widely spoken.

Many Congolese are Christian, mostly Roman Catholic. There are a small number of Muslims. Traditional African religious beliefs are widespread and are based on respect for one's ancestors, a belief in a universal spiritual force, and belief in magic and charms.

Living in the Congo

The Republic of Congo is, by African standards, a relatively well-off country, although its economy is hampered by international debt and the high cost of living. Its chief mineral resource is petroleum, production of which soared during the 1980s. Oil now accounts for 90 percent of all exports. Trying to spread the national income more evenly, the government is developing hydroelectric projects, paper mills, and rubber plantations. Pointe-Noire is a major industrial center and remains the sole seaport for vast areas of central Africa. Affected by the heavy rains, the roads are poor. Therefore the rivers provide the most important method of transporting people and goods. Slow riverboats steam upriver to Bangui (bahng-GEE), the capital of the Central African Republic, when the water levels are high during the rainy seasons.

The rain forests yield precious hardwoods, such as mahogany and limba, and softwoods, such as *okoumé* (oe-KOO-mae). Cash crops include sugarcane, peanuts, palm oil, cocoa, and coffee. Yields are low and foods have to be imported. Most people produce just enough food for themselves and for the local market, growing corn, cassava (a starchy root), rice,

and plantains (cooking bananas). Plots of land are farmed communally by a clan (a group of people who have the same ancestor) or a village as a whole. About half of the workforce works on the land. Few live in the more remote areas of rain forest.

Older housing is made of mud, timber, and thatch, or, in the case of the Baka, branches and leafy fronds. Concrete and metal roofing are also a common sight. Brazzaville has modern high-rise buildings and tree-lined streets, although fighting between political rivals has seriously damaged many buildings in recent years.

Artists and Musicians

The area of the Congo Basin is the center of a visual art tradition that is one of the finest in Africa. The Basin is famous for its beautiful masks and carved statues. African masks and statues had a major impact on European artists in the early 1900s. In the Republic of Congo during the colonial period, art was taken up with renewed passion, with new mediums being explored. The Poto-Poto School of Painting in Brazzaville, founded in 1951, made its mark on the art world as far away as Paris and New York.

In the field of music, too, the Republic of Congo was famed for its drumming and ritual dancing, for its bells, flutes, and horns. Early European visitors sketched musicians at the royal court of Loango. Modern Congo pop music, often in the Lingala language, is heard in Brazzaville. The sound may seem to be a world away from the medieval kingdoms of Kongo and Loango, but it does remain part of the same ancient tradition.

Food in the Republic of Congo is typical of the region. Palm oil is widely used for cooking. Cassava root is mashed into a porridge and served with a little spicy meat. Cassava leaves may be boiled up to make a dish called *saka-saka* (sah-kah SAH-kah), and palm cabbage may be eaten as a salad. *Piri-piri* (pih-ree PEE-ree) chicken is seasoned with pepper. Peanuts are ground into a thick paste. The rivers provide perch (a type of fish), and coastal waters and lagoons yield oysters, shrimp, shark, skate, swordfish, grouper, red tuna, and tarpon. Fish is often smoked, grilled, or stewed. In the forests, animals are still widely hunted for food. Monkeys, snakes, warthogs, and antelopes may all end up in the cooking pot.

Life expectancy is low, with men living to an average of only forty-five years and women to forty-nine years. A major problem is the lack of clean water in rural areas, which gives rise to parasitic and intestinal diseases. Malaria is common, and AIDS is widespread.

Education is compulsory for ten years. About 70 percent of adult males can read and write, while only 44 percent of women can, since girls are often kept from school to work on the land and in the house.

For a circumcision ritual at Mbomo in the northwest, a boy's face is painted white. He belongs to the Kota people, who also live across the border in Gabon (see GABON).

Women, however, do play an important economic role as market traders.

Most of the Republic of Congo's peoples wear informal, nontraditional dress. The men wear shirts or T-shirts with trousers. The women may wear Western clothes or skirts and dresses of printed cotton.

DJIBOUTI

THIS LITTLE COUNTRY LIES JUST ABOVE THE HORN OF AFRICA, which is a great hook of land that extends from eastern Africa south of the Red Sea.

Djibouti has an arid landscape covered by sparse scrub and bare rock. The plain bordering the Djibouti coast rises to a series of mountain ranges in the north, reaching 6,652 feet (2,028 meters) at Mount Mousa. Assal, a salt-encrusted lake in the central region, is the lowest point in Africa, at 471 feet (144 meters) below sea level. Bleak, volcanic plateaus dot the south.

CLIMATE

Djibouti is one of the hottest countries on Earth, with temperatures between June and August reaching 113°F (45°C). A summer wind blows sand in from the desert in the south. Cooler weather arrives in October and lasts until March.

Average January temperature: *78°F (26°C)*

Average July temperature: *96°F (36°C)*

Average annual precipitation: *5 in. (13 cm)*

A camel caravan, or trading expedition, brings salt to the Djibouti coast. It was the salt trade that first brought people to the harsh deserts of the region.

On the Horn of Africa

There was never much to attract settlers to the land of Djibouti (ji-BOO-tee). There was some pasture for livestock, but it was mostly thorn and scrub and not farmland. However, valuable salt, left as a residue once the burning sun evaporated the waters of Lake Assal (ah-SAHL), did beckon. And, from about 4,500 years ago, so did trade with Egypt and the Middle East in frankincense and myrrh (fragrant resins, used in making incense and perfumes). There was also a natural harbor, where the seaport of Djibouti stands today, positioned between the Indian Ocean and the Red Sea. This region was one of the world's busiest trading routes.

The north and much of the interior of the country was settled in about 250 B.C.E. by people from the Arabian peninsula, the ancestors of today's Afar (uh-FAHR). The Afar are also known as the Danakil (DAH-nah-kihl) people. About 350 years later the south was settled by Somali (soe-MAH-lee) people, who founded the Issa (EE-sah) subgroup there. Both peoples were mostly nomadic, wandering the arid zones with their herds in search of pasture.

The faith of Islam arrived from Arabia about 825 C.E., and during the Middle Ages Djibouti became part of a trading network that extended down the coast to the islands of East Africa and eastward to India. The chief goods were spices, minerals, and slaves. By the fourteenth century, an Islamic state called Adal had emerged. At the height of its power it stretched from the east of the Ethiopian Plateau, eastward to the Red Sea and the Indian Ocean. It took over the Red Sea trade and challenged Ethiopia, the powerful state that then dominated northeast Africa (see ETHIOPIA).

Over time it was the French who finally came to rule what is now Djibouti. They purchased the port of Obock (oe-BAWK) from the local Afar sultan in 1862 so that they could dominate the shipping lanes to the south when the Suez Canal opened in 1869. In 1884 they purchased Tadjoura (tah-JOO-rah), also from a local Afar sultan, and by 1888 their possessions in the region

FACTS AND FIGURES

Official name: *Jumhouriyya Djibouti*

Status: *Independent state*

Capital: *Djibouti*

Other towns: *Tadjoura, Ali Sabih, Dikhil, Obock*

Area: *8,957 square miles (23,199 square kilometers)*

Population: *650,000*

Population density: *73 per square mile (28 per square kilometer)*

Peoples: *60 percent Issa (Somali); 35 percent Afar (Danakil); 5 percent other, including French, Arab, Sudanese, Indian*

Official languages: *Arabic and French*

Currency: *Djibouti franc*

National day: *Independence Day (June 27)*

Country's name: *Djibouti takes its name from its chief seaport, on the southern shores of the Gulf of Tadjoura.*

had become the colony of the French Somali Coast, or French Somaliland.

The capital was Djibouti, which became a very important seaport for the Suez trade. A railway was soon built, linking the coast with Addis Ababa (AHD-dis AH-bah-bah), the Ethiopian capital. By 1957, French Somaliland had home rule, but in 1967, 60 percent of the population voted against independence, since France offered aid and economic and military security. Violent riots followed the election. Ethiopia demanded Afar territory in northern Djibouti because so many of the Afar

Time line:	People from Arabia, ancestors of Afar, settle the north	Issas settle the south	Islam arrives	Rise of Islamic state of Adal	French control port of Obock
	ca. 250 B.C.E.	ca. 100s C.E.	825	1300s	1862

This photograph shows poor basket makers outside their shelter of poles and skins in 1930. They were camped in part of Djibouti, at that time capital of French Somaliland.

people already lived across the border in Ethiopia. After a decade of terrorism and political unrest, the country finally became independent as Djibouti in 1977.

The new state was still heavily involved with France. The presence of French Foreign Legion troops, which retained a major base in Djibouti, probably helped to deter Ethiopia and Somalia from meddling.

Djibouti faced huge problems. The closure of the Suez Canal from 1967 to 1975 during conflicts between Egypt and Israel had seriously affected the continuance of Djibouti as a seaport. War flared across the Horn of Africa from the 1970s into the 1990s (see ETHIOPIA, ERITREA, and SOMALIA). The railway was temporarily closed. Refugees poured across Djibouti's borders. There was a severe drought in 1984 and disastrous flooding ten years later.

Unrest continued, as the Afar of the north and central regions clashed with the Issa of the south. The main sources of the conflict have been political and economic inequalities. The Issa predominate as city dwellers. This has put them in a position to take the best jobs and dominate the country's politics. Djibouti became a one-party state in 1981, ruled by the People's Assembly for Progress. Guerrillas of the Front for the Renewal of Democracy, supported by Afar villagers in the northeast, fought against the government until a peace agreement was reached in 1994.

Djibouti Today

The chief problem facing Djibouti today is a common one in Africa. The colonial borders have created a state that makes little sense politically, culturally, or economically.

About 5 percent of Djibouti's population are of French, Yemeni Arab, Sudanese, or Indian origin. The remainder is made up of Afar people (about 35 percent) and the Somali Issa (about 60 percent). Both these groups are Muslim.

Afar who still live the traditional desert life, herding cattle, goats, sheep, and camels, have to be tough. They are great admirers of physical stamina and bravery. Their history is a fierce one; at one time women would only marry a man who could prove

French Somaliland created	French Somaliland gains home rule	Independence as Djibouti	Multiparty constitution, civil war between Afar and Issa peoples	Peace agreement
1888	**1957**	**1977**	**1992**	**1994**

that he had killed an enemy. They are a tall, lean people. The women wear black scarves around their heads and brown wraparound dresses, while men wear a white kilt, the *sanafil* (SAH-nah-feel). Many carry old-fashioned daggers and weapons. Encampments comprise houses in which mats are placed over a framework of sticks. Herds provide milk and meat.

Despite the hostility between the Issa and Afar, Issa who have not moved into the city follow a similar way of life. They too are a tall, tough people who build homes from mats and sticks. Herders live a nomadic life, traveling in extended family groups. Issa women wear colorful scarves around their heads and wraparound dresses, and the men wear long tunics. The Issa as a whole are divided into clans (people who claim descent from a common ancestor), and each of these is headed by a chief.

Many people have left the harsh desert regions for the city or for other lands. The port of Djibouti is now home to over 80 percent of the country's population. Most wear Western clothes and have abandoned the customs of desert living. However, their fierce loyalty to their own ethnic group remains.

The economy today still depends on the duty-free seaport, which is modernizing to compete for Red Sea trade. The railway link with Ethiopia remains important because there are only 50 miles (80 kilometers) of surfaced roads. Industry, based in the port, is on a small scale. Some

market gardening and salt mining is possible, and fishing takes place along the coast. Herding dominates the interior of the country. There is a booming trade in a narcotic known as *qat* (KAHT). Qat leaves are chewed throughout large areas of northeast Africa.

Families must pay for their children's education, which is not compulsory. There are no universities. Less than two-thirds of men and less than one-third of women are literate.

Only rich city dwellers have access to good health care. On average, women live to an age of fifty-two, men to forty-nine. Most of the female population undergo a genital cutting procedure (see SOMALIA). Many children die in the first five years of life (164 per 1,000). AIDS is a major problem in the seaport.

Afar women belonging to the family of the sultan of Tadjoura in their traditional finery, which includes elaborate headdresses, nose rings, earrings, necklaces, bangles, and finger rings.

EGYPT

EGYPT IS A NATION IN NORTHERN AFRICA, bordered in the north by the Mediterranean Sea and in the east by the Red Sea.

Most of Egypt is desert, the eastern edge of the vast Sahara that stretches across northern Africa. Only 3.5 percent of the country is cultivated and permanently inhabited. This fertile land lies along the banks of the Nile River and in the Nile Delta.

The Nile Valley is rarely more than 10 miles (16 kilometers) wide and has high cliffs on either side. In the north the river opens out into the flat, marshy Nile Delta.

The Arabian Desert, in the eastern part of the country, is a wide plateau bordered by a jagged mountain ridge. The Sinai Peninsula in the far northeast is also desert. It contains Egypt's highest mountain, Gebel Katherina at 8,652 feet (2,637 meters). The desert to the west of the Nile is a flat plain, covered by shifting sand dunes. It contains the Qattara Depression, 436 feet (133 meters) below sea level.

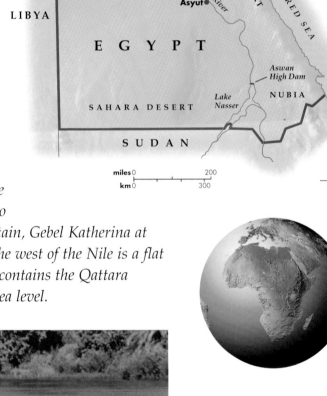

For thousands of years the Nile River has been the main highway linking Upper and Lower Egypt. These Egyptians are traveling in a felucca, a boat with a triangular sail.

136

Ancient Egypt

Egyptian civilization began over eight thousand years ago, when people living beside the Nile River began to plant crops. By 5000 B.C.E. they had learned how to keep sheep, goats, and cattle. Around 3100 B.C.E. the peoples of northern and southern Egypt (EE-jipt) joined together to form one nation ruled by a pharaoh.

The rich, powerful kingdom of ancient Egypt survived for the next three thousand years. Egyptian farmers grew wheat, barley, fruits, and vegetables and caught fish and waterfowl. They invented irrigation technologies to help them irrigate their fields, such as the *shaduf* (shuh-DOOF), which scooped water from rivers. Egyptian women harvested flax from the riverbanks to spin and weave into fine linen cloth. In cities and towns

FACTS AND FIGURES

Official name: *Jumhuriyat Misr al-Arabiyah (Arab Republic of Egypt)*

Status: *Independent state*

Capital: *Cairo*

Major towns: *Greater Cairo (Cairo plus adjoining Giza, Shubra al-Khaymah, and Hilwan), Alexandria, Port Said, Suez*

Area: *386,660 square miles (1,001,449 square kilometers)*

Population: *66,900,000*

Population density: *173 per square mile (67 per square kilometer)*

Peoples: *99 percent Arab and Berber; also Nubians, Bedouins, Greeks, Armenians, Italians, French*

Official languages: *Arabic*

Currency: *Egyptian pound*

National day: *Anniversary of the (1952) Revolution (July 23)*

Country's name: *The word Egypt comes from the ancient Greek word Aegyptos, based on Egyptian words Hik Up Tah, meaning "House of the Spirit."*

CLIMATE

Egypt's climate has just two seasons: hot, from May to October, and cool, from November to April. However, in the southern desert, temperatures can rise and fall dramatically within twenty-four hours. In April and May, sandstorms and hot, dry southerly winds blow in from the Sahara, damaging crops. Throughout Egypt little rain falls, except along the Mediterranean coast.

	north	south
Average January temperature:	*61°F (16°C)*	*77°F (25°C)*
Average July temperature:	*90°F (32°C)*	*95°F (35°C)*
Average annual precipitation:	*8 in. (20 cm)*	*it may not rain for several years*

Egyptian artisans made fabulous jewelry from gold, silver, and precious stones. Egyptian builders constructed massive pyramids, temples, palaces, and tombs, and Egyptian artists created beautiful carvings, statues, and wall paintings. People from neighboring nations envied the Egyptian people and their rich, splendid civilization. The Egyptians themselves claimed that their land had been blessed by the gods.

Time line:	First farming villages built	Egypt united under one ruler called a pharaoh	Nubia (land south of Egypt) conquered; new lands farmed	Greek kings and queens rule Egypt
	ca. 5500–3100 B.C.E.	**3100–2181 B.C.E.**	**2055–1650 B.C.E.**	**332–330 B.C.E.**

Pyramids and Mummies

Pyramids are massive monuments containing burial chambers. They were built in ancient Egypt between about 2686 and 1550 B.C.E. to house the bodies of dead pharaohs and other wealthy, powerful people. Farmworkers built pyramids (sometimes as a way of paying their taxes) during the annual Nile flood season, when it was impossible to work on their sodden farmland. Workers used simple stone and wooden tools and lots of muscle power. Stone blocks for building each pyramid were quarried near the site, rolled up long ramps made of earth, and hauled into position. The shape of the pyramid was important; it represented the slanting rays of the sun or possibly a sloping stairway leading up to heaven.

The ancient Egyptians believed that peoples' spirits could only survive after death if their bodies survived as well. They preserved dead bodies by removing the inner organs, drying the flesh and bones with natron (a chemical salt), and wrapping the remains in linen bandages. Wealthy families also paid for fine, painted cases or for stone caskets called sarcophagi (singular: sarcophagus) to put the preserved bodies, or mummies, in. Mummies were buried in tombs decorated with pictures of the dead person and their family enjoying themselves in the afterlife.

Scrolls of papyrus (reed paper), called Books of the Dead, were buried alongside mummies to guide dead peoples' souls. They often portrayed the dead person—here, a scribe and his wife.

A Parade of People: Romans, Copts, Arabs, Ottomans

The Romans had conquered Egypt by 30 B.C.E. and made it part of their empire. To them, Egypt's chief asset was its rich annual harvest of grain, which they shipped across the Mediterranean Sea to feed the people of Rome. Under Roman rule, Egypt's arts and beliefs survived, although they were sometimes blended with Greek and Roman ideas and designs. However, heavy taxes on rural produce made many Egyptians poor. They left their

Egypt part of the Roman Empire	Coptic Christian church established	Arabian Muslims control Egypt; Arabic language and Islam introduced to cities	Fatimid dynasty controls Egypt and founds Cairo	Farmers and herders from Arabia settle throughout Egypt
30 B.C.E.–395 C.E.	**ca. 100 C.E.**	**639–952**	**952–1171**	**ca. 1000**

farms and moved to the cities to find work. This caused food-supply problems and less income from taxes for Rome. Eventually, the power of the Roman Empire declined, and Roman rule ended in 395 C.E.

Long before then, around 100 C.E., monks, nuns, and hermits, seeking solitude for prayer and meditation in Egypt's eastern desert lands, established the Christian church in Egypt. Egypt, especially Alexandria, became home to one of the first civilizations based on Christian beliefs and values. This civilization became known as "Coptic," after the language spoken by people in northern Egypt. Coptic clergymen played a leading part in important religious debates and controversies at a time when the organized

The head of the Coptic Church is known as the Pope. He is shown here leading a service in a Coptic church in Lower (northern) Egypt.

Christian religion was first taking shape. They sent missionaries to Ethiopia and other nearby lands.

In 639 Muslim soldiers from Arabia arrived in Egypt and took control of the government. They settled in northern Egypt's towns and cities and introduced the Arabic language and their new faith, Islam. These changes had little immediate impact on the ordinary country people of Egypt, who continued many of their Coptic traditions until around 1000.

Until 952, Egypt was governed by rulers based in Damascus, now in Syria, and Baghdad, now in Iraq. Then the Fatimids, a new Muslim dynasty from the area that is now Tunisia, conquered Egypt and founded a new capital city at Cairo (KIE-roe). The Fatimids greatly encouraged learning and the arts by building schools, colleges, libraries, and mosques. Cairo's massive city walls and gates were completed around 1080. Expert artisans produced exquisite works of art, especially pottery, woodwork, fine fabrics, and carved rock crystal. The Fatimids fell from power in 1171, after Saladin, a commander in the Syrian army, took control of Egypt.

In 1250, groups of Mamluks (Turkish war captives and slaves, originally brought to Egypt to serve as soldiers in Arab armies) seized control. Like the Fatimids, they reformed the government and encouraged

Mamluk soldier-slaves take control of Egypt	Egypt becomes part of Ottoman Empire	Muhammad Ali Pasha becomes viceroy of Egypt under Ottoman rule	Muhammad Ali defeats Ottomans; becomes hereditary ruler of Egypt	Suez Canal opens
1250	**1517**	**1805**	**1841**	**1869**

learning and the arts. Egypt was a rich prize for any foreign conqueror, and in 1517 it was captured by Sultan Selim I, who ruled the mighty Ottoman Empire based in Istanbul, Turkey.

Europeans Arrive

In 1798 the French army invaded Egypt as part of Emperor Napoléon Bonaparte's bid to conquer the Middle East. The French were driven out by Ottoman and British forces in 1801, and in the confusion that followed, an Albanian officer in the Ottoman army, Muhammad Ali, seized power. In 1805 he became viceroy (a sultan's deputy) and for the next thirty-five years led Egyptian soldiers to fight against the Ottoman sultan's enemies.

Muhammad Ali began ambitious programs to modernize Egypt's farmland, government, and economy, but his successors failed to complete them. The opening of the Suez Canal in 1869 brought trade and toll money to Egypt. However, these were not enough to pay off the country's massive debt. The debt was the result of ambitious projects planned by Egypt's ruler, Khedive Ismail, to modernize his country and buy freedom from Egypt's overlords, the Ottoman emperors in Istanbul. Ismail's projects led to economic crisis. A group of army officers rebelled, and the Ottomans dismissed Ismail from power. Great Britain had helped pay

French army officers negotiate a peace treaty in 1801 with a senior official in the Ottoman government of Egypt known as the Grand Vizier.

Egyptian nationalist revolt against Ottoman rule	Great Britain rules Egypt	Arabic kings rule Egypt	Revolution; Egyptian army deposes King Farouk	Egypt becomes a republic	Gamal Abdel Nasser becomes president
1881–1882	1883–1922	1922–1952	1952	1953	1954

Egypt's debt and was anxious to protect the Suez Canal, so it seized control of Egypt's government from 1883 to 1922.

Independence and After

From 1922 to 1952 Egypt was ruled by Arabic kings, although Great Britain still claimed rights to protect the Suez Canal. In 1952 the Egyptian army staged a revolution, and the next year Egypt became a republic. In 1954 army leader Gamal Abdel Nasser seized power, and in 1956 he nationalized the Suez Canal.

Nasser introduced a series of major reforms for the government and economy based on socialist ideas. They gave the state power to control farming, industry, transportation, and power utilities. In many ways Nasser's grand projects, including the Aswan (ah-SWAHN) High Dam, were similar to those of the strong, centralized government of the pharaohs of thousands of years ago. Nasser received aid and political support from the former Soviet Union. This was a time of tension between Egypt and its neighbor Israel. In 1947 the United Nations (UN) was anxious to provide a homeland for European Jews after the persecution and genocide the Jews had suffered in the 1930s and 1940s. The UN therefore decided to divide the region of Palestine (roughly the same area as modern day Israel) into Jewish and Arab states. The region of Palestine had been part of Jewish kingdoms in ancient times but then came under Muslim control for more than a thousand years until it was conquered by the British in 1917.

Palestine's inhabitants were Arabs. Like many other Arab and Muslim states, Egypt opposed the division of Palestine and the foundation of the Jewish state of Israel. Instead, it supported the Palestinians' rival claim to establish an independent homeland on the same soil. This dispute led to four major wars and many lesser battles between Egypt and Israel from the 1950s to the 1970s.

Nasser died in 1970 and was replaced by Anwar as-Sadat. He too introduced major changes, this time designed to ally Egypt more closely with the Western, capitalist world. He expelled Soviet advisors and sold nationalized industries to private firms. He made friends with European Union countries and the United States. He also took part in negotiations with Israel, which ended in a peace agreement in 1979. Sadat's pro-Western policies angered Muslim extremists, who assassinated him in 1981. Today Sadat's policies are continued by President Muhammad Hosni Mubarak, who has ruled since Sadat died. Egypt faces many problems, but it is a country that is widely respected, both for its ancient heritage and as one of the leaders of the modern Muslim world.

Many Peoples, One Land

The people of Egypt have many different origins. They are descended from ancient Egyptians, Roman conquerors, Coptic Christians, Arab invaders, Turkish soldiers, and Armenian, Greek, and Italian traders. All these peoples and their cultures have mingled together over the centuries to

Nasser nationalizes Suez Canal	Six-Day War with Israel	Aswan High Dam completed. Anwar as-Sadat becomes president	Egypt-Israel peace treaty	Sadat assassinated; Muhammad Hosni Mubarak replaces him	Government faces opposition from Muslim fundamentalists
1956	**1967**	**1970**	**1979**	**1981**	**1985 onward**

Bedouin women from the Western Desert region of Egypt spinning and weaving wool. Bedouin artisans are famous for the fine woolen carpets they make.

create a unique civilization. There are also Nubians (black Africans) in the south, together with Bedouins (BEH-dwihns, Arabic-speaking pastoral nomads) and Berbers (BUHR-buhrs, who are descended from the ancient native people of north Africa) in the deserts.

Egyptians (except the Berbers and some Nubians) speak Arabic and share customs and traditions that have slowly developed over the past two thousand years. In big northern cities separate communities of Armenians, Italians, and Greeks speak their own languages plus Arabic. The ancient Coptic language still survives, but it is now used only in religious ceremonies.

Ever since ancient times Egyptian society has been divided between rich and poor. Today a few wealthy, powerful people run the country, with top jobs in the army and the government. The civil service and the skilled professions are run by a small, well-educated middle class. Ordinary working people, who make up the bulk of the population, have the right to vote and take part in politics, but they have little chance of joining the ruling elite or having any real power. Economists estimate that between one-third and one-half of the families living in Egypt's big cities should officially be classed as poor.

Religion in Daily Life

About 90 percent of the people in Egypt follow the Sunni branch of the Islamic faith. Islam was first brought to Egypt from Arabia between 639 and 642 C.E. and plays an important part in Egyptian life today. It influences everything from education to what women wear in public. It is also the basis for family and community life.

The main Muslim festival is Eid al-Fitr, which takes place the day after the end of Ramadan, a month-long period of fasting between dawn and dusk. Eid al-Fitr celebrations can last for several days. People feast and give presents, and families get together for reunions.

The religion of Islam teaches that there should be no difference between God's laws and the ordinary, everyday laws governing a country. Because of this, there has been a long tradition of Muslim political activity in Egypt. Muslim political leaders have campaigned to make all aspects of Egypt's government fit in with *Shariyah* (SHAH-rih-yah), Muslim holy law.

Peaceful Islamic organizations play an important part in Egyptian politics. Their members are mainly from a broad spectrum of social classes in the big cities. They hope to solve Egypt's social and economic problems by returning to traditional Muslim virtues, such as hard work and strict morality, and by ending greed and corruption in public life. There are also several illegal Muslim organizations, mostly in the countryside, that use terrorist tactics such as bombings and murder to try to overthow the government, drive away non-Muslims, and frighten ordinary people into supporting their cause.

About 8.5 percent of Egyptians are Coptic Christians. Since the nineteenth century they have worked as government

Muslims saying prayers in the street in Alexandria, one of Egypt's largest cities. Wherever they are, devout Muslims pray five times a day at specific times.

officials; today many are among the most well-educated people in the country. Many are doctors, lawyers, professors, and business managers. Another 1.5 percent of the population, mostly Greeks, Armenians, and Italians, belong to different branches of the Christian church.

This house in Upper (southern) Egypt is decorated with pictures of plants, animals, and the Kaaba, the holy black stone that stands in the Muslim holy city of Mecca.

Stories on Walls

Muslims believe that it is their religious duty to make a pilgrimage to the holy city of Mecca in Saudi Arabia at least once in their lives. In Upper (southern) Egypt, villagers who have made this pilgrimage often decorate the outside of their houses with illustrations of their journey and of the Muslim holy places they visited along the way.

kin. Wives were valued chiefly as housekeepers and as mothers of sons. They had to be very careful not to bring shame on their husbands by defying customs or being outspoken. Usually they had to wear a veil in public. The practice of female genital cutting has always been common (see SOMALIA). Even today, most Egyptian women undergo this procedure when young.

After the 1952 revolution, educational opportunities for women improved, and women began to seek careers outside the home. In 1979 the government introduced a law for women that sought to improve women's rights in marriage, divorce, and child custody. However, some of these new rights were abolished in 1985 after campaigns by Muslim politicians who strongly disapproved of them.

The Role of Women

Traditionally most Egyptian men believed that women were inferior—physically, morally, and intellectually. Women were expected to obey their male relatives and to avoid all contact with men who were not

During the 1990s, women made up 12 percent of the workforce. About half of working women have low-paying jobs in offices, factories, hospitals, and service industries such as cooking and cleaning. There are also many female doctors,

Young women students at Cairo University. Education is creating new opportunities for women in Egypt; many now have successful professional careers.

teachers, university lecturers, and engineers. Women writers often discuss the changing roles of women in their work.

Rural and Urban Life

Most of Egypt is uninhabited. Over 96 percent of the population lives on just 4 percent of the land, in the Nile Valley and Delta region. About half the population lives in the countryside and half in the cities. However, recent population growth has led to unemployment in the countryside. More and more people are moving to the cities in search of work. Some districts of Cairo (the capital city) and the Nile Delta are among the most crowded places on earth, with over 4,000 people per square mile (10,360 per square kilometer).

In the countryside most people live by farming. Farmers grow corn, wheat, rice, barley, onions, potatoes, lettuce, cucumbers, tomatoes, beans, eggplants, and many kinds of fruit, including mangoes, oranges, lemons, figs, grapes, and dates. Modern irrigation provides a steady water supply year-round, instead of just a few months, as in the past. This enables farmers to harvest several crops from one plot of land each year. There are large government-planned plantations where bulk crops such as cotton and sugarcane are grown. The crops are later transported to factories, where they are processed.

Egypt's population is growing rapidly—by almost 3 percent a year—and about four out of every ten people are under age fifteen. This has led to problems. Although the Nile Valley and Delta regions have fertile soil, the amount of land suitable for

Grain crops, fruits, and vegetables grow well in Egypt's warm, damp, fertile soils. These women farmers have grown a large crop of rice.

This family-run village bakery in the Nile Delta region supplies a traditional specialty, large round loaves of flat bread that have been baked in a brick oven.

farming is small, and Egyptian farmers cannot grow enough to feed everyone. Egypt has to import about half its food.

The government gives large subsidies to farmers and manufacturers to reduce the price of food so that ordinary workers in towns can afford it. Even so, the poorest families have to spend about 75 percent of their income on food. When the government tried to remove these subsidies in the past, violent protests arose in many cities and towns.

For ordinary people, Egyptian food is simple. They cannot afford luxuries of any kind. Many fruits, flowers, and vegetables grow quickly in the rich, black, moist soil beside the Nile River, and even the flowers and the leaves of some flowering plants can be consumed. *Melokhia* (meh-LOE-kih-yah) is a soup made from the leaves of mallow flowers. Favorite foods include soups and stews made of meat broth and vegetables: usually onions, peppers, tomatoes, carrots, zucchini, and other squashes. Soups and stews are eaten with rice or bread. Hearty

dishes made of dried beans, lentils, or chickpeas are also popular. *Ful medames* (FOOL meh-DAHMS) are cold beans with olive-oil dressing, eaten with hard-boiled eggs; *lablabi* (lah-BLAH-bee) is chickpea broth poured over dried bread. Strong flavorings, such as cumin, chili, and garlic, are added to many dishes. Lamb, goat, rabbit, beef, and chicken are available, but only wealthy people can afford to eat much meat. For dessert there is fresh fruit; sweet, sticky dates; and syrupy pastries made from semolina and nuts. Muslims are forbidden to drink alcohol by their holy book, the Koran. Tea, mint tea, and coffee are all widely drank, along with fresh fruit juices and cold carbonated drinks.

In cities people work in shops, offices, factories, hotels, restaurants, schools, and hospitals, as well as for the government and the tourist trade. Some have jobs in the media and transportation. Textiles are

Bourek (BOO-rehk): Spicy Meat in Pastry

You will need:

1 pound (400 grams) ground beef or lamb
2 onions
1 teaspoon (5 grams) ground cumin
1 pinch chili powder or 1 chopped green chili
¼ teaspoon each of salt and pepper
2 large eggs
cooking oil
pastry made from a mixture of 1 lb (450 grams) flour and 8oz (225 grams) margarine

Chop the onions and fry them in oil over a low heat until soft; add meat and stir until thoroughly cooked. Add cumin, chili, salt, and pepper. Stir and cook two or three minutes more. Roll out the pastry fairly thinly and cut into circles about 6 inches (15 centimeters) across.

Beat the eggs and stir half the beaten eggs into the meat filling mixture. Place two large spoonfuls of mixture on one half of each pastry circle; fold over to make a half-moon shape. Stick pastry edges together with more beaten egg; brush with any leftover beaten egg.

Bake on a greased baking sheet in a hot oven at around 350°F (180°C) for about twenty minutes or until the pastry is crisp and golden. Served with lettuce, it's an Egyptian favorite since ancient times. This quantity will serve four people.

the most important industry: Egyptian cotton is among the finest cotton in the world. Other factory-made products include iron and steel, chemicals, fertilizers, cement, sugar, tobacco, and cottonseed oil. In the deserts there are oil and natural gas wells along with iron and manganese mines. Many men also work as builders, laborers, and truck drivers or seek whatever temporary work they can.

Egypt's Economy

Gasoline and cotton are Egypt's major exports; the government also earns income from tourism and the Suez Canal. Egypt's economy is boosted by money sent home by millions of migrant workers who have left Egypt to live and work abroad. However, Egypt has to rely on foreign aid

Egyptian children sometimes work alongside their parents in small family workshops. This boy is helping his father repair an old, badly damaged car.

147

Aswan High Dam

The Aswan High Dam, located on the Nile River in southern Egypt, is one of the world's largest structures. Completed in 1970, it is 2.3 miles (3.7 kilometers) long and 364 feet (111 meters) high. The reservoir behind the dam, known as Lake Nasser (NAH-suhr), is 310 miles (500 kilometers) long and 6 miles (10 kilometers) wide. The water stored there generates about 25 percent of Egypt's electric power. The dam took ten years to build, at a cost of $1 billion. The government hoped it would also serve as a political symbol, displaying Egypt's power and prestige.

The Aswan High Dam was designed to regulate water supplies to the Nile Valley and Delta and to irrigate desert land so that it could be used for farming. It has not been a complete success. Changes in water flows and levels have caused many problems: mineral salts have built up in Nile waters and in the irrigated land; there has been severe soil erosion in the Nile Valley; and valuable fisheries in the Nile Delta have been destroyed.

Many important archaeological remains have been buried under water or damaged by dampness and salt. Other remains had to be moved to safety, away from their historic sites. There has been a human cost as well; because of the dam, over 100,000 Nubian men, women, and children from Egypt and Sudan had to be resettled in new villages far from their original homes.

to survive. It has few natural resources, is running short of usable land, has high unemployment; sprawling, polluted cities; a fast-growing population (in spite of government family-planning programs); and a serious housing shortage. Many years of war and costly public projects, such as the Aswan High Dam, have also weakened its economy.

Education and Health

Ever since the Middle Ages, the city of Cairo has been a center of learning for students from many Muslim lands. Its famous Al-Azar University, founded in 970 C.E., is the oldest in the world. Traditionally, only students from wealthy, upper-class families were able to get a good education. Before the 1952 revolution, only 20 percent of the population could read and write. Today there is free education for all.

By law, all children from the ages of six to twelve are supposed to attend school, but Egypt's rapid population growth has made it difficult to provide enough schools. Because they are kept at home by their families, often to work, about one in eight children does not attend school. Today about half the adult population can read and write.

Egypt is not a very healthy place to live. In the past its people suffered badly from diseases carried by Nile River water, such as schistosomiasis, dysentery, and intestinal worms, as well as chest diseases caused by sand and dust from the desert. Many experience weakness caused by the lack of nourishing food. Waterborne diseases are still quite common, especially in the countryside. To try to fight them, the Egyptian government requires that newly qualified doctors work in country areas for at least two years. Since the revolution,

Teachers and pupils at an elementary school. Like many Egyptian women, girls wear long, loose clothes with a floral pattern and cover their hair with veils or scarves.

government doctors and nurses have provided free medical care. Life expectancy has improved to about sixty years for men and sixty-four years for women.

Houses and Homes

Many families in the Nile Valley and the Delta still live in village houses built of sun-dried mud brick. These are small and very simple, with just two or three dark rooms. Sometimes they have a roof terrace, where families can seek fresh air under a shady awning. Larger homes have tall vents, like chimneys, that draw cool air down into living rooms, creating a refreshing breeze. Some larger homes have courtyards. Newer village homes are made of cement blocks or concrete, with groved iron roofs. Without air-conditioning, which ordinary families cannot afford, homes can be stiflingly hot in summer.

In cities people live in apartment buildings several stories high. Many of these have been hastily and illegally built to meet the urgent need for housing among workers moving to the cities. Many are unsafe and some have collapsed. About 200,000 families live in loosely constructed homes made of wood, metal, and cardboard perched on the roofs of apartment buildings. In Cairo half a million people seek shelter in mausoleums (burial chambers) in city cemeteries. Overcrowding like this seriously depletes water supplies and damages drains. There is not enough public transportation for everyone, and garbage is not collected often enough.

Nomadic Bedouin men sit around a fire in the center of their camp. Most Egyptian men spend free time with other men, talking, smoking, and drinking coffee.

Bedouins and Berbers: Desert Nomads

The Bedouins and Berbers were traditionally nomads, moving from oasis to oasis in search of grass and fresh water for their herds of camels, sheep, and goats. Nomad homes were tents woven from camel hair and furnished with rugs. Each nomad group fiercely defended its own territory, and rival groups occasionally feuded.

Today some Bedouins and Berbers are still nomads, but many, encouraged by government programs, have moved to settle on small plots of farmland. Many Bedouin families that lost their grazing grounds when the Aswan High Dam was built live in overcrowded government settlements in Nubia (southern Egypt). Climate changes and drought in the desert have made it increasingly difficult for nomads to survive. Some Bedouins have found employment in

the tourist industry as hotel workers and guides; others work in big cities doing whatever jobs they can. Many Berbers have also moved to towns in search of work.

The Nubians: A Displaced People

Until recently, the Nubian (NOO-bee-uhn), or black African, people of southern Egypt lived by farming small plots of land and herding cattle. After the Aswan High Dam was built, many thousands of Nubian families were resettled in new villages, far from their original homes. They disliked the modern cement-block houses they were offered, and they hated being cut off from

Nubian people have lived in southern Egypt for generations. Thousands of years ago, they ruled a rich kingdom and traded with the ancient pharaohs.

ancient family ties. The government offered them work on sugarcane plantations, a huge change from their previous way of life. As a result, many migrated to big cities, where they still live today.

Monuments and Music

Egyptian people are proud of their country, which is a fascinating mixture of old and new. Egypt has a rich heritage of ancient buildings, from pharaohs' pyramids to Ottoman palaces, built by strong, centralized governments as declarations of their power or as monuments to their beliefs and ideas. The city of Cairo alone has over six hundred fine Muslim monuments, including the world-famous Ibn Tulun Mosque, built around 876 C.E.

This beautiful mihrab (MEE-rahb)—niche facing Mecca— and minbar (MIHN-bahr), or pulpit, where the preacher stands, are in the mosque of al-Nasir Muhammad in Cairo.

More recently, massive engineering projects, such as the Suez Canal and the Aswan High Dam, have continued the same impressive trend.

Yet Egyptian culture consists of more than grand government buildings. A long tradition of popular music and dance flourishes, although this is being replaced by music heard on radios and televisions.

Music is not just entertainment; it forms part of many family and religious celebrations. Egyptian weddings have always been joyful occasions, celebrated with singing, dancing, and feasting among the newly married couple's family, neighbors, and friends. Men and women do not usually dance together in public. Songs tell stories or pass on ancient ideas and beliefs. Traditional instruments dating back more than two thousand years include flutes and oboes, lutes, castanets, and terra-cotta drums.

EQUATORIAL GUINEA

THIS ATLANTIC REPUBLIC is made up of two regions: Mbini, a mainland territory, and Bioko. Bioko includes the large island of that name, which lies in the Bight of Biafra, 100 miles (160 kilometers) northwest of Mbini, and the island of Pagalu, which lies some 400 miles (640 kilometers) southwest of Bioko.

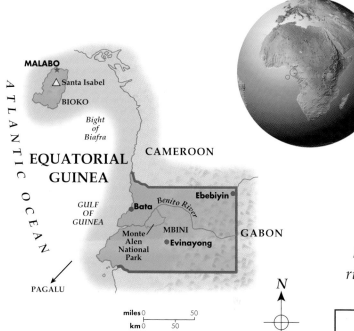

Mbini is a land of equatorial rain forests broken by savanna. A narrow coastal plain rises to plateau country, which averages about 2,000 feet (610 meters) above sea level. Fast-flowing rivers on their way to the Atlantic Ocean cross the coastal plain. The Benito River is the chief waterway. Bioko is formed from three inactive volcanoes and rises to over 9,865 feet (3,007 meters) at Santa Isabel. It has crater lakes, mountains, forests, and a rich soil for agriculture.

CLIMATE

The climate is hot and humid, with equatorial rainfall. The heaviest rains fall on Bioko between July and October. In Mbini the rainiest months are April to May and October to December.

	Bata (Mbini)	Bioko
Average January temperature:	*79°F (26°C)*	*77°F (25°C)*
Average July temperature:	*79°F (26°C)*	*77°F (25°C)*
Average annual precipitation:	*94 in. (239 cm)*	*78 in. (198 cm)*

Atlantic Coasts

The earliest people in Mbini (uhm-BEE-nee) were probably distant relatives of the Baka and Gyeli peoples who still live in Cameroon. They hunted wild animals and gathered food deep in the rain forests. None live in Equatorial Guinea (GIH-nee) today.

Over thousands of years, peoples from the Bantu (BAN-too) language group spread out over western and central Africa. About two thousand years ago, they became ironworkers as well as farmers and fishers. By 1100 C.E. some of them, such as the Ndowe (ehn-DOE-wae), had settled the Mbini region. By the 1200s another Bantu group, the Bubi (BOO-bee), had left Mbini in their canoes to settle on the island of Bioko (bee-OE-koe). The most powerful of

152

the Bantu peoples proved to be later arrivals, the Fang (FAHN-jee), who intermarried with the Ndowe and soon dominated the Mbini region. They were renowned for their weapons of copper and iron, which included swords, spears, and throwing knives.

In 1470 Portuguese ships, exploring routes around the African coast, discovered Pagalu (pah-GAH-loo), and two years later the navigator Fernão do Po was in Bioko, which he named Formosa. However, the island was later named Fernando Póo (the Spanish form) after him, and this remained its name until independence.

The Portuguese, trading in slaves, ruled the islands until 1778, when the islands were ceded to Spain as part of a wider exchange of territories. An outbreak of fever drove new Spanish settlers from the country within a few years. The islands were neglected until 1821, when Spain agreed to allow the British navy to use the

FACTS AND FIGURES

Official name: *République de Guinea Ecuatorial*

Status: *Independent state*

Capital: *Malabo*

Other town: *Bata*

Area: *10,830 square miles (28,050 square kilometers)*

Population: *450,000*

Population density: *42 per square mile (16 per square kilometer)*

Peoples: *In Mbini: 80 percent Fang; 20 percent others, including Kombe, Balengi, Bujeba, Ndowe, Bayele. On Bioko: Fang, Bubi, Fernandinos (mixed descent), others*

Official language: *Spanish*

Currency: *CFA franc*

National day: *Independence Day (October 12)*

Country's name: *Guinea was the European name for a large part of the western coast of Africa. It may be derived from Djenné, the old trading center, now in Mali, or from the Ghana empire, or it may come from the berber word aguinaw, meaning "black man."*

port of Santa Isabel (now Malabo) on Fernando Póo. It became the base of a policing operation designed to enforce the recent ban on the transatlantic slave trade. Many freed slaves settled on the

Malabo, the country's capital, is a town of about 35,000 people on the island of Bioko. Palm trees, shuttered windows, balconies, and grooved iron roofs are typical features of Malabo's streets.

Time line:	Bantu peoples settle in Mbini	Bubi start settlement of Bioko	Portuguese settle islands	Islands ceded to Spain	Mbini borders established	Spanish Territories of the Gulf of Guinea founded as colony
	ca. 1100 C.E.	ca. 1200	1500s	1778	1900	1909

island, and their descendants are still known as Fernandinos.

By 1844 the Spanish had returned to Fernando Póo, and in the 1880s cocoa was planted on the island. It brought in huge profits, and for a time the island was the world's leading cocoa producer. However, many west African lands followed the Fernando Póo example and soon exceeded Bioko's cocoa production.

Under Spanish Rule

By 1909 both mainland and islands had become a colony called the Spanish Territories of the Gulf of Guinea, normally referred to as Spanish Guinea. The Spanish knew little of the mainland and its interior. They faced fierce opposition from Fang warriors, who were finally suppressed by Spanish troops in the 1920s.

Labor for the cocoa plantations was imported from west African countries, including Nigeria and Cameroon. Working conditions were so appalling that the League of Nations (the forerunner of the United Nations) set up an investigation into working practices on Fernando Póo in the 1920s.

Spanish Guinea became a Spanish overseas province in 1959, and it was not until then that the indigenous population gained civil rights as citizens. However, this was not enough for the Fang of Mbini, who demanded independence and took their case to the United Nations, who put pressure on Spain. Home rule was granted to what was now called Equatorial Guinea in 1963.

Macías Nguema and After

In 1968 Equatorial Guinea did achieve full independence. Relations with Spain rapidly turned sour. Spanish settlers were harassed and quickly left the country.

In 1973 the country became a one-party state under Francisco Macías Nguema, who had been elected president in 1971. His clan (a group descended from the same ancestor), the Mongomo, and his people, the Fang, were favored above the Bubi and other minorities. Macías Nguema closed the country to the outside world. A reign of terror was unleashed on the country, as political opponents were imprisoned and possibly as many as fifty thousand were executed. As much as 30 percent of the population fled to neighboring lands. The economy collapsed and Macías Nguema reintroduced forced labor.

By 1979 even Macías Nguema's closest allies had had enough. He was overthrown by his nephew, Teodoro Obiang Nguema Mbasogo, and executed. Political prisoners were released, and normal life gradually returned to Equatorial Guinea. However, economic problems, attempted coups, and political unrest continued. Multiparty elections were held in 1993, and Obiang Nguema was reelected. Observers from other countries agreed that the voting was not fair. The same accusations were made of the 1996 election, at which Obiang Nguema's Democratic Party of Equatorial Guinea claimed nearly 98 percent of the vote. Today the people of Equatorial Guinea still suffer human rights abuses. As many as 100,000 live in exile.

Home rule	Full independence	Dictatorship under President Francisco Macías Nguema	Macías Nguema overthrown. Teodoro Obiang Nguema Mbasogo takes his place	Multiparty elections; Obiang Nguema reelected
1963	**1968**	**1973**	**1979**	**1993 and 1996**

Life Goes On

The economy of Equatorial Guinea still depends principally on the export of cocoa and coffee, as well as on fisheries and on logging for *okoumé* (oe-KOO-mae) and *akoga* (oe-KOE-gah) wood in the rain forests of the mainland. Farming, fishing, and forestry production have never recovered to the levels achieved before the dictatorship of Macías Nguema. The country is heavily dependent on aid from Spain.

The potential for improvement is there, however. The soil of both Bioko and Mbini is fertile, and oil and natural gas reserves off the coast of Mbini promise future wealth. Bioko, with its spectacular mountain views and pretty, old colonial buildings, might

Forest conservation on the equator is hard work. Two workers in the Monte Alen National Park stop for a break and some refreshment provided by forest fruits.

become a tourist destination. However, it seems likely that any new wealth will line the pockets of the ruling class or international business rather than those of the ordinary people.

Most ordinary people still struggle to survive, working the cocoa and coffee plantations for wages. Others farm their own small plots of land to feed their families or supply the local markets with cassava, yams, and plantains (large cooking bananas). Seventy-seven percent of workers still farm the land, while only 2 percent of the population work in industry, mostly in food or timber processing. They work in Malabo (mah-LAH-boe), which is the capital, on the island of Bioko or Bata (BAH-tah), the chief town of Mbini.

As the economy collapsed during the years that followed independence, so did education. Many pupils simply stopped

At the hilltop town of Evinayong, southeast of Bata, a schoolgirl clutches her math books. After years of strife and economic collapse, education is now a national priority.

155

Leopard Men

Fang beliefs revolve around a fear of witchcraft and a faith in the power of rituals and healers to battle against the forces of evil. If anyone suffers bad luck or illness, they believe it to be the work of "leopard men," who are said to take part in human sacrifice and cannibalism. Witches and evil spirits can, however, be overcome by special rituals carried out by members of a secret society and by healers, who counteract the spells of the leopard men.

by the Fang immigrants from the mainland, who have been eager to be near the country's center of political power. Bioko is also home to Fernandinos, descendants of the liberated slaves of the 1820s. There are also a number of *Crioulous* (kree-OO-loos), or Creoles, people of mixed descent. The population of Pagalu is said to be descended from Africans who were shipwrecked there in the 1400s. The minority peoples of the mainland coast, mostly fishers, farmers, and laborers, include the Bujeba (boo-JAE-bah), Balengi (bah-LEHN-gee), Kombe (KOHM-bae), and Mabeya (mah-BAE-yah). Some of these have mixed with the Fang, who now make up over 80 percent of the national population.

going to school. However, education is now an official priority, and the literacy rate is 89 percent for men and 67 percent for women.

Life expectancy in Equatorial Guinea is estimated to be fifty-two for men and fifty-seven for women. Even this figure is an improvement since the colonial era; in 1960 the average age at death was only thirty-seven.

The Roman Catholic Church, despite persecution after independence, has a very large following. African traditional beliefs survive among the Bubi, who celebrate harvest festivals, and they are especially strong among the Fang, who have maintained a powerful fascination for spirits and witchcraft.

The Bubi, the original Bantu-speaking settlers of Bioko, now live mostly in the mountains in the north of the island. During colonial times, the Spanish favored the Bubi, but now they have been greatly outnumbered

A teenager carries a basket on her back as she hurries to work in the fields near Ebebiyin in the far northeast of the mainland region.

With expert skill, a basket maker bends a tangle of tough, springy fronds into a neat, closely woven basket. Basketry is a traditional craft of Equatorial Guinea.

Music and Dance

Traditional musical instruments of Equatorial Guinea include drums, varieties of stringed instruments, and wooden xylophones, as well as the sanza *(SAHN-zah), a small instrument whose bamboo keys are plucked with the thumb. The sanza is popular in many parts of central Africa and is known in places as a* likembe *(lih-KEHM-bae).*

Dance plays an important part in the lives of many people. It serves as religious ritual as well as entertainment and celebration. Dancers may cover their bodies with white powder or wear elaborate costumes of grass, feathers, leopard skin, and monkey fur. One famous dance is the balélé *(bah-LAE-lae), which involves leaping and shaking. Another energetic dance is the* ibanga *(ee-BAHN-gah), the national dance of the Fang.*

Because of the country's economic troubles in the 1970s, few musicians could buy the instruments and recording equipment needed to produce successful pop music like the music that was being produced in Nigeria, Mali, and the Democratic Republic of Congo. Musicians made do with patched-up acoustic guitars and improvised percussion instruments. The pop music scene is based in Malabo and is strongly influenced by the popular rhythms of Cameroon and the Democratic Republic of Congo. The most successful band of the post independence years, Desmali, originally came from Pagalu.

The Fang, who also live in Cameroon and Gabon (see CAMEROON and GABON), were originally farmers who followed a slash-and-burn cultivation pattern, clearing the forest and planting cassava, yams, and corn. They lived in temporary villages. Since the values and social structures of the countryside are often not relevant in urban life, modern Fang society has been greatly altered by members working on plantations and settling permanently in towns. Though many still have traditional scarring on their cheeks, a common practice across many parts of Africa, they often wear Western-style clothing.

Languages heard in Equatorial Guinea include Spanish and a Portuguese dialect among the population of Pagalu. The Bubi, Fang, and their neighbors speak their own languages, which belong to the Bantu group, as well as Spanish.

ERITREA

ERITREA IS A SMALL COUNTRY IN NORTHEASTERN AFRICA, bordering the Red Sea.

Eritrea's central highlands reach a height of 9,882 feet (3,012 meters) at Mount Soira. A steep escarpment drops sharply toward the dry, hot, narrow coastal plain. The western lowlands slope down to the Sudanese border; here the land is dry savanna.

CLIMATE

Summer temperatures in the coastal region can rise to 120°F (49°C), and the average annual rainfall is only 8 inches (20 centimeters). In the central highlands it is much cooler and wetter. In the western lowlands the summer can be as hot as on the coast, but the winter temperatures are cooler.

Average January temperature: *78°F (26°C)*
Average July temperature: *94°F (34°C)*
Average annual precipitation: *21 in. (53 cm)*

A Diversity of Peoples

The peoples of Eritrea (ehr-uh-TREE-uh) come from a variety of backgrounds, with very different religions and patterns of living. Some early inhabitants came from the Nile River area; many, particularly between the 800s and 600s B.C.E., came from southern Arabia. They formed separate groups and lived in small kingdoms.

Early in the 100s C.E. the peoples of Eritrea came under the control of the Aksum (AHK-soom) kingdom. Aksum, in the highlands of Ethiopia, was the most important state in the Red Sea region by the 500s (see ETHIOPIA). It controlled commerce over an enormous area, trading in slaves and a variety of goods, including frankincense, gold, myrrh, and ivory. Converted by missionaries from Syria, the rulers of Aksum had become Christian and spoke the language of Geez (GIH-ehz). The power of Aksum began to decline during the 600s because it was losing control of trade in the Red Sea region to Muslim Arabs. Plus, slash-and-burn agriculture had exhausted the land, and farmers were producing less food.

From the 600s to the 1300s, cultural influence in Eritrea came from the Middle

East instead of Ethiopia. Some coastal regions were inhabited by Muslims, particularly the Massawa (mah-SAH-wah) region. From the 1300s onward, kings in Ethiopia occasionally made efforts to control the coastal region, but during the 1500s the Ottoman Turks took over Massawa. In the highlands, the Ethiopian kings installed

These Christians are celebrating Maskal, or the Finding of the True Cross, an important Orthodox festival celebrated each September in both Eritrea and Ethiopia (see ETHIOPIA).

FACTS AND FIGURES

Official name: *Hagere Erta (State of Eritrea)*

Status: *Independent state*

Capital: *Asmara*

Other towns: *Massawa, Asseb, Keren*

Area: *45,300 square miles (117,327 square kilometers)*

Population: *4,000,000*

Population density: *88 per square mile (34 per square kilometer)*

Peoples: *50 percent Tigrinya; 30 percent Tigre; also Saho, Afar, Kunama, Nara*

Official languages: *Arabic and Tigrinya*

Currency: *Nafka*

National days: *Liberation Day (May 24); Martyrs Day (June 20); Start of Armed Struggle (September 1)*

Country's name: *Italians named the country Eritrea, based on ancient Greek references to the Red Sea as the Erythrean Sea.*

military garrisons and appointed royal officials, but in the 1700s the kingdom of Tigray (TEE-grae) replaced the Ethiopians as the dominant force.

Colonial Rule

The completion of the Suez Canal in 1869 (see EGYPT) began a period of intense European rivalry for northeastern Africa. Italian missionaries had awakened Italian interest in Eritrea. By 1882 the Italians controlled Asseb, and by 1885 they controlled Massawa as well. They used Eritrea as a base from which to attack Ethiopia but were defeated by the Ethiopians in 1896.

The Italians established the boundaries of modern Eritrea. They encouraged

Time line:	Eritrea is part of Aksum Empire	Coastal regions inhabited by Muslims	Turks on Red Sea coast	Tigray kingdom dominates Eritrean highlands	Treaty of Uccialli gives Italy control over Eritrea
	ca. 100–600 C.E.	ca. 600–1400	1500s	1700s	1889

settlers from Italy to grow crops such as oranges and olives for export. They built the capital of Asmara (ahz-MAHR-uh), a few schools, and the railroad between Asmara and Massawa.

In 1935 the Italians once more used Eritrea as a base from which to launch an attack against Ethiopia, this time successfully. In 1941, during World War II, the Allied forces defeated Italian troops in northeast Africa, thus ending Italian rule of Eritrea, Ethiopia, and Somalia. The British then controlled Eritrea for nine years. They, however, had no long-term interest in the area and agreed to Eritrea forming a federation with Ethiopia in 1952, a move that appeared to be supported by the majority of Eritreans. This arrangement was supposed to ensure that Eritrea had its own parliament and control over its internal affairs.

The War against Ethiopia

Ethiopia soon began to interfere in Eritrea's internal affairs. It declared Amharic (the language of Ethiopia) the official language of Eritrea in 1960 and two years later dissolved the Eritrean parliament and took direct control of the country. In 1961 the Eritreans began a thirty-year armed struggle against Ethiopia to regain their independence. The war was fought by the Eritrean People's Liberation Front (EPLF) and other groups. One-third of the population of Eritrea had to leave their homes to seek refuge either in other parts of the country or abroad. Eventually an alliance of the EPLF and several Ethiopian opposition groups defeated the Ethiopian regime, and in 1991 the EPLF entered Asmara and liberated the country. In the 1993 referendum, almost the whole country voted for independence.

Many refugees began returning, but in May 1998 a new conflict between Eritrea and Ethiopia started. There had been a number of economic and political disputes between the two countries since independence. During June 1998 there were air strikes on both sides. By 1999 efforts to settle the conflict had failed.

Eritrea Today

The long years of war against Ethiopia meant that there were few resources available for developing Eritrea's economy and social services. The government is now working hard to improve education and health care for people and to develop industries and agriculture.

During the 1980s massive efforts were made to reduce illiteracy. Education is free in government schools, but in rural areas children are often kept home to work on the land. During their first five years of schooling, children learn Tigrinya, Arabic, and English. Tigrinya (tih-GREEN-yah) and Tigre (TEE-grae) use the same Geez alphabet, which has over two hundred characters, each representing a different sound.

During the war with Ethiopia, medical assistants were trained to work in primary health care (the prevention of illness). Once the country was at peace, health services improved dramatically. The life

Ethiopians defeat Italians at battle of Adawa	Italians attack Ethiopia	British rule begins in Eritrea	Federation with Ethiopia	War with Ethiopia begins	EPLF liberates Eritrea	Eritreans vote for Independence
1896	1935	1941	1952	1961	1991	1993

Half the population of Eritrea are Tigrinya-speakers who live primarily in the southern part of the central highlands. They live mainly by farming in the fertile valleys and keeping a few animals. The Tigrinya are Christian, mostly belonging to the Orthodox tradition (see ETHIOPIA), although some are Catholic.

The second largest group of people (around 30 percent) are the Tigre. Tigre-speakers live farther north than the Tigrinya and are Muslim.

There are also nomads on the coastal plains. These include the Saho, Afar, and Rashaida peoples. In the western lowlands live the Kunama (koo-NAH-mah) and

Since independence, education has been a priority for Eritrea. These Muslim girls are enthusiastic about their schooling, and the makeshift classroom provides shelter from the sun.

expectancy is fifty-four years for men and fifty-eight for women.

The main towns in Eritrea are linked by tarred roads. Some areas of the country are inaccessible because of the mountainous terrain. Buses are the most common form of transportation.

The war hurt the agriculture and industry of Eritrea, and the crucial port of Massawa was badly damaged. Most people survive by herding goats, sheep, or cattle and by subsistence agriculture, growing sorghum, millet, barley, and teff (a cereal grass). Industry is being revived, helped by investments from returned refugees, who took their money with them when they fled, and by the use of workers who learned valuable mechanical skills during the war. The industries tend to be focused around Asmara, the capital. There is an oil refinery at Asseb, and oil companies are surveying the Red Sea for deposits.

The Christian Church

In the Tigrinya areas of Eritrea, the largest building in the village is the church. The holiest part of the church is where the tabot *(TAH-boe), a container for sacred texts, is kept. During important festivals, such as Timkat, which celebrates the baptism of Jesus, the tabot is brought out of the church and is carried in processions. Colorful umbrellas are held over the priests. The priests carry large decorative crosses and conduct the services in the ancient language of Geez. The religious art of Eritrea shows people facing forward. Only evil people are shown in profile.*

This Kunama village is in a remote part of the western lowlands. Everyone is watching a game of soccer, a popular sport with Eritreans.

The Coffee Ceremony

Whenever Eritreans visit each other, they drink coffee, and the small stove for making coffee, the fernello *(feh-NEH-loe), can be found in even the smallest house. Coffee is always made by a woman. The coffee beans are roasted over the fernello. Once roasted, they are ground with a pestle and mortar. The coffee is put into a metal pot, water is added, and the coffee is boiled on the fernello. When the coffee is ready, it is strained and served with sugar. Usually the coffee is boiled three times. Each serving becoming weaker as more water is added. A courteous guest samples all three servings.*

Nara (NAH-rah) peoples. Most of these people are Muslim, although a few, particularly among the Kunama, retain their traditional animist religions. (Animists believe that natural objects around them, such as rivers and mountains, have sacred properties.) On special occasions Christian women wear long white dresses and scarves. The dresses are heavily embroidered on the sleeves and bodice and around the neck and bottom. Muslim women dress modestly, keeping their arms covered. Many women of all religions wear colored shawls over their everyday clothes.

Before the war against Ethiopia, Eritrean women had very few rights. However, during the war many women fought side by side with the men. Now their position has greatly improved; they can go to school, work where they choose, own property, borrow money, and have a say in whom they will marry. However, the practice of female genital cutting is still widespread (see SOMALIA).

The staple foods of Eritrea are *kitcha* (KEE-chah), a thin, unleavened bread made from wheat, and *injera* (ihn-JEH-rah), a spongy pancake made from teff or sorghum. The ingera forms a sort of plate onto which stew made from meat and/or vegetables is put. Pieces of ingera are torn off from around the edges, and from other injera pancakes, and dipped into the stew.

Life in the Towns

Asmara was hardly damaged by the war. It has well-planned, tree-lined avenues with wide pavements. In the residential areas large villas, built by the Italians, can be glimpsed behind high walls. People work for the government or in industry, or they may sell goods in the crowded markets or on the street. The streets are lively with pavement cafes, bars, and restaurants. The cafes serve cappuccino (a strong coffee) and pasta as well as more traditional food. For entertainment, people can go to the movies or the theater.

Massawa is the main port. The buildings there are a mixture of whitewashed Italian, Turkish, and Egyptian styles. Inhabitants may work in the port or in factories. The town is full of little alleyways with lively bars and cafes.

Life in the Country

The many country people live in small stone houses roofed with grooved iron, together with perhaps an ox, a donkey, or hens. The women and girls work in the house, preparing the bread and pancakes, collecting water, and making coffee for afternoon visits.

Hilly and rocky, much of the land is difficult to cultivate. Between February and May, men plow the land and build small stone walls in terraces on the hillsides to prevent the soil from running off. During the main rains, from June to September, seeds are planted and crops weeded. Harvesting extends from September to December. In January and February the people build houses and enjoy family celebrations such as weddings.

Many people in the driest areas of Eritrea, such as the coastal plain and the western lowlands, are nomads. They move from place to place with large herds of sheep or goats, their belongings loaded on camels. They live in tents made from woven mats and poles. In some areas people may grow crops in the rainy season, but they will move up to the highlands with their animals when the weather becomes very hot.

The Rashaida people are nomadic Arabs who live on the coast near Massawa. The Rashaida breed camels, which they use to carry their belongings from place to place.

Glossary

AIDS: *a*cquired *i*mmuno*d*eficiency *s*yndrome, a normally fatal disease often passed on by sexual intercourse. It is caused by the virus HIV (*h*uman *i*mmunodeficiency *v*irus), which attacks the body's ability to resist disease and infection.

Allied forces: soldiers belonging to the countries (including Great Britain, France, the USA, and the Soviet Union) who fought together against Germany, Italy, and Japan during World War II (1939–1945).

bodice: the part of a garment that covers the waist up to the bust.

capitalism: an economic system in which land, factories, and other ways of producing goods are owned and controlled by individuals, not the government.

cassava: a plant with fleshy tuber roots, used as a food.

castanets: a musical instrument made of two little disks of wood or metal that are clicked together to produce a sound.

centralist: supporting a strong central government rather than a regional or federal system of government.

CFA franc: franc de la Communauté Financière Africaine (franc of the African Financial Community). This is a unit of currency shared by various African countries that were formerly French colonies.

chiefdom: a territory ruled by a chief.

coalition: a temporary alliance between political parties or groups of people.

Cold War: the period of tension between 1945 and 1990, when the USA and its allies repeatedly clashed with the communist Soviet Union and its allies (now the Russian Federation and its neighbors).

communism: a theory that suggests that all property belongs to the community and that work should be organized for the common good.

  communist: someone who believes in the theory of communism.

confederation: a political grouping; an alliance.

corruption: dishonest behavior by people in public office.

coup: a change of government brought about by force.

delta: a triangular area of marshy land where a river flows into the sea.

dissidents: people who disagree with a government or a policy.

equatorial: relating to regions close to the equator, an imaginary line drawn on maps around the middle of the world. A typical equatorial climate is hot and wet all year-round.

escarpment: the steep face or cliff of a mountain ridge or range of hills.

European Union: an alliance of European nations committed to economic union and closer political integration. It developed out of the European Economic Community (founded in 1957).

exploitation: making use of, taking advantage of, or profiting unfairly from something.

fly whisk: a stick with a tuft of animal hair or similar material, used to brush away flies in hot countries.

forerunner: an earlier version; a predecessor.

home rule: self-government without full independence.

human rights abuses: human rights are conditions that many people believe are deserved by all human beings, such as freedom, equality, or justice. Abuses are acts that deny people such rights. Examples of abuses might include torture, censorship, or imprisonment without trial.

indigenous: relating to a people who were born within a country or a region as opposed to being immigrants or settlers. Also *aboriginal* or *native*.

inflation: rising prices, with currency falling in value.

left-wing: pursuing radical, progressive, or socialist politics.

malnutrition: suffering or ill health caused by a poor diet or insufficient food.

mercenary: a hired soldier; someone who fights for money.

millet: a hardy cereal crop grown for food, drink, and fodder.

missionary: someone who is sent to bring a religious faith to nonbelievers. Christian missionaries often work as preachers, teachers, doctors, and nurses.

nationalize: to make something the property of the nation or state.

parliament: a democratic legislature or assembly.

persecution: oppressing and harassing people for their beliefs.

pharaoh: the ancient Egyptians' name for the god-king who ruled them.

plantain: a fruit similar to the banana. It is a staple food in many tropical countries.

protectorate: a territory that is given the protection of a more powerful state. In the colonial period in Africa the "protection" was often just a ploy by European countries to achieve political control of the territory.

regime: a form of government.

republic: a country in which power rests with the people and their elected representatives. A president usually heads a republic.

rumba: one of several dances that has complex rhythms in 2/4 or 4/4 time. The rumba comes from Cuba but has its roots in the music of African slaves.

savanna: a grassland dotted with trees and drought-resistant undergrowth.

secession: the act of breaking away from a larger country or federation.

slash-and-burn (cultivation): the practice of felling trees and clearing the ground by burning, then using it for crops for a few years before moving on.

socialism: a political theory in which the community or government controls land, property, industry, and money, and organizes them for the good of all the people.

sorghum: a grain crop commonly grown in hot countries.

Sunni: a group within the worldwide Muslim community, comprising about four out of every five Muslims. Sunni Muslims aim to follow the Sunnah (the example of prayer and good behavior set by the Prophet Muhammad) in their daily lives.

Further Reading

Internet Sites
Look under Countries A to Z in the Atlapedia Online Web Site at
    http://www.atlapedia.com/online/countries
Look under country listing in the CIA World Factbook Web Site at
    http://www.odci.gov/cia/publications/factbook
Look under country listing in the Library of Congress Country Studies Web Site at
    http://lcweb2.loc.gov/frd/cs/cshome.html

Congo, Democratic Republic of
Heale, Jay. *Democratic Republic of the Congo.* Tarrytown, NY: Marshall Cavendish, 1999.
Lerner Publications, Department of Geography Staff. *Zaire in Pictures.* Minneapolis, MN: Lerner
    Publishing Group, 1993.
Roberts, Mary Nooter, and Allen F. Roberts. *Luba.* New York: Rosen Group, 1996.
Okeke, Chika. *Kongo.* New York: Rosen Group, 1997.

Congo, Republic of
Okeke, Chika. *Kongo.* New York: Rosen Group, 1997.

Djibouti
See web sites mentioned above

Egypt
Diamon, Arthur. *Egypt: Gift of the Nile.* Minneapolis, MN: Dillon Press, 1992.
Kallen, Stuart A. *Egypt.* San Diego, CA: Lucent Books, 1999.
King, John. *Bedouin.* Orlando, FL: Raintree Steck-Vaughn, 1993.
Loveridge, Emma. *Egypt.* Orlando, FL: Raintree Steck-Vaughn, 1997.
Pateman, Robert. *Egypt.* Tarrytown, NY: Benchmark Books, 1995.
Saman, Anzhil Butrus. *Egypt.* Tarrytown, NY: Marshall Cavendish, 1993.
Tenquist, Alasdair. *Egypt.* Detroit, MI: Thomson Learning, 1996.
Watson, Jane. *Egypt, Child of the Nile.* Champaign, IL: Arcade Books, 1997.
Weber, Valerie, Julie Brown, and Robert Brown. *Egypt.* Milwaukee, WI: Gareth Stevens: 1992.
Wilkins, Frances. *Egypt.* Broomall, PA: Chelsea House, 1998.

Equatorial Guinea
Aniakor, Chike C. *Fang.* New York: Rosen Group, 1996.

Eritrea
Gilkes, Patrick. *Conflict in Somalia and Ethiopia.* Glendale, CA: New Discovery, 1994.

Index

Page numbers in *italic* indicate illustrations.

Page numbers in *italic* indicate illustrations.